The Power of Choices

By

Tracy A. Medling

An excerpt from her breakout inspirational publication:

"Stories from the Well"

Coming winter, 2011

Published in the United States by HW Publishing, a subsidiary of House of Walker Publishing, LLC, New Jersey

Library of Congress Control Number: 2011914218
Copyright © 2011 by Tracy A. Medling
The Power of Choices/Tracy A. Medling
ISBN: 978-0-9834762-1-4

Foreword

It is so wonderful to see another precious woman receive the gift of healing and restored whole again, by the power of our Lord and Savior Jesus Christ.

As you read the words of this book, Tracy brings you into her life of pain, heartache and searching for the truth. This book will encourage you, strengthen you and let you see a heart set free from the tragedy of abortion.

Pati Adams
Executive Director for a crisis pregnancy center
Speaker, working in the Pro-life arena for 12 years
But most of all, Forgiven, healed and Set Free from
my past 3 abortions.

Special Thanks
to

Emily Stimson and Bethany Brohinsky for their contributions to the content and graphic design for the cover of my first published work ~

Claire Culwell, Gianna Jessen, Melissa Ohden, Jill Stanek, Jason Jones, Beth Moore, Joyce Meyer, James and Betty Robison, Women of Faith, Joseph Prince, and Patty Massey-Cadwell
I owe you more than I can say for your testimonies and ministries, helping me see the Preciousness of God's Grace and helping me apply it to the specifics of my life.

My undying Gratitude to
Linda Cochrane and Pati Adams
who were pivotal in my final victory over the shame, the guilt and the degradation of my abortion.

May God bless each of you richly in the mercy of His manifold Grace.

Table of Contents

Foreword

Special thanks

Introduction

Dedication

Acknowledgments

Introduction

Life is full of Choices. We all make hundreds of choices every day. It is an integral part of being human and living every day life. Freedom of choice is a privilege and a power we are gifted with by God Himself. It is a freedom that we take for granted in many ways, because most of the choices we make seem to be pretty inconsequential: coffee or tea, white or rye, highway or back roads...in the grand scheme of things, these choices' impact can be pretty minor most of the time. But there are some choices that are crucial to our future. Some choices that we make have eternal impact, and nothing we do from that moment on will ever be the same. They become a pivot point that every move we make traces back to. It can be something positive that sparks a whole new creative endeavor for hundreds, or even millions of people. But one choice can also be so cataclysmic, that it drives the destruction of generations for years to come. So it is with this area of choice. Nowhere is this truth so passionately personified than in the abortion debate. In no other arena can the result of our own and others' choices be so final, cause such crippling pain and set a series of unintended consequences in motion, like ripples in the ocean on one end of the world becoming a tsunami on others. I realize the abortion issue is very controversial and raises contention from many sides and perspectives. I can only share mine, why I believe what I believe, and how I feel. Take what you can out of the sharing.

You may begin reading this with completely different view points than mine on the topic. Please read this anyway. If nothing else, it will help you understand why people who have differing views on the topic are unwilling to – actually completely unable to – accept that there can be any "common ground" on abortion.

If you are not yet facing this decision, you need to read this as well. If you heed its counsel, it can keep you from being in the position to make this horrible choice in the first place. It may also give you the ability to be a resource to a friend who may be faced with this decision in the future.

If you are reading this because you or someone you love is facing this choice in life, and are struggling with what path you should take, know that you are not alone. Many, many women have been where you are: fearful, panicked, excited, wondering, terrified, hopeful, angry, unsure – the range of emotions are overwhelming and seem to flip-flop with no apparent rhyme or reason. Read this. Talk to people who aren't necessarily invested in the decision you will make – those who do not gain or lose financial advantage in what you will choose. Talk to people who have been where you are and can tell you their story and how their choices affected them. Informed decision, made with *all* the pertinent details filled in before you choose, is critical to the process.

CareNet, BirthRight, and dozens of other organizations and websites can show you what some will be unwilling to tell you because it goes against what they want you to choose. Inform yourself. Even You Tube can be a great source in information! (Be careful though, having a trusted friend with you might be a good idea, as some of the stuff can be pretty graphic and your emotions cannot be trusted right now.)

If you are reading this and you have already acted on the decision to abort, it is probable you are having a hard time with the results you were never told about ahead of time. It is possible that you feel like there's no way to endure the regret, shame, second-guessing, and tears that you wish you weren't shedding right now. Please hear me: this book was written by someone just like you for you. I was there. But thanks to others who went there before me, I can honestly say I am free from the pull of hopeless grief and the relentless regret I felt for so many years. Read this and know...."

Above all, know that someone, somewhere is praying for you. You are not alone. You are not the first one to face these choices and you won't be the last. Know that you are loved deeply, more than words can say. And this Love will never, never leave you nor forsake you. There are many choices in life, and you have the Power to make them. Let this one be a choice for Life.

Dedication

To

Jordan Elizabeth

and

Hunter Grace

until I see you face to face...

and

to every unexpectedly pregnant woman who is wondering what they should do in the next few days, please hear my heart: Regret is a very poor substitute for Peace and Joy.

Life is full of choices. The right choice is always found in Life and Integrity

Never forsake them and they will guard your path.

Acknowledgments

I want to thank my husband, Steve and my children and grandchildren who make my time here on earth worth living, and to God Who blessed me with each of them. I want to thank Michelle for encouraging me through each step of the publishing process. To Tom, Joe, Scott and Lynn who gave me helpful tips and support along the way. I am very grateful to Sr. Marie Andre', the other sisters, and the girls at the Academy of the Holy Family who gave me my first opportunity to share my story publically, and for Sr. Mary Mark who first told me about naming my aborted and miscarried children.

I want to thank Life Today, Gateway Church, Beth Moore, Jimmy Evans, Joyce Meyer (and many others) for the books and assorted media you've made available for Biblical instruction. You and they have been a great help to me.

My gratitude to my pastor, Sonny Stimson, who introduced me to Care Net, Brian Daly, who organizes our local "40 Days for Life" calendar every year, and to Father Joseph Tito who tirelessly defends the pre-born, in everything he does.

To all the volunteers and staff everywhere who have adopted these children and taken up the fight - thousands of women and men all over the world who have the courage to share their lives and stories and strength in speaking engagements, on You Tube, and anywhere else they can

For Life.

The Power of Choices

"I call heaven and earth to witness this day against you that I have set before you life and death, the blessings and the curses; therefore choose life, that you and your descendants may live."
Deuteronomy 30:19

When I first became aware of a local event called 40 Days for Life, I was a 44-year-old grandmother of two. One of my grandchildren was walking and running and eating and out in the open where I could see him, and the second was growing and eating and moving and developing the outer characteristics that would enable *us* to be able to tell, in a few short months, that she was a girl with the most beautiful blue eyes and grin, easily startled by loud noises and capable of some incredibly urgent screams, just for not getting what she wanted at the moment. (She is carrying on a three-generation tradition, after all! ☺) And as I began to write this, my third grandchild - my second granddaughter - was moving, growing and doing gymnastics – or was it water ballet? – usually at the times my daughter-in-law was trying to sleep. She was not due to be born for another two months, but she was absolutely making her presence felt. She promises to be a very active little girl! My grandchildren, Jason, Emily, and Natalee are the second generation of victory walking on this earth in my own personal life. My children are the first. They were almost not born.

A few years ago, during that local 40 Days for Life campaign, I was given the opportunity to share my experience publically for the first time. This nation-wide event is a time for prayer, education and outreach to help people understand the importance of defending life - personally and in the public arena. It incorporates a 40-day time period in which local people organize activities ranging from round-the-clock prayer vigils and walking in front of abortion clinics, to pro-life rallies and educational events, in conjunction with Pro-Life organizations, abortion alternative centers like BirthRight and CareNet, and churches. The articles of conduct the participants agree to in conjunction with these events mandate supportive and non-violent interaction with everyone the participants come in contact with, no matter what the setting or provocation.

I was invited to speak, along with other women and pro-life organization representatives, to all the girls then attending my old high school, for a school-wide assembly during the 2007 campaign in my area. All the girls in the school got involved. Some made posters; another created not one, but two powerful Power Point slide presentations set to music, others wrote letters and poetry – they were all so creative and passionate about their choice for life. It was wonderful! I was honored to be asked to be a part of it. But it was not without pain. My part in this event was not one of clinical facts on human development. It was not one of a conscience-free idealist who has always followed that path of defending life as the gift and miracle it is. I was the messenger of warning - and hope. I had an abortion 28 years before this event, while I was attending this very school. I would be sharing the before and after, the road that brought me to a pit of fear and regret at too young an age – and the consequences that were far steeper than I could have imagined in the beginning. I also came to share the hope of true freedom of God's Grace and forgiveness that lifted me out of that pit and healed my heart.

During one of my occasional visits to see some of the resident nuns, I had been talking with one of the sisters who had been just a novice when I was attending the school. We had become friends then and kept in touch intermittently through the years. I recently had revealed to her some of my experiences in connection with this – the worst decision of my life, bar none. I also shared how, now that Jesus had taken away the shame and self-condemnation from my heart I wanted nothing more than to be a lighthouse of sorts, warning the girls away from rocks they should never have to run aground on. I don't think I had ever seen her so excited as when the idea for me to come to the school as a speaker for this event crossed her mind and lit up her face ☺ There was no condemnation in her eyes or heart, just the embrace of compassion. I jumped at the opportunity. Jesus has healed me, and, like the blind man, or the leper who is now free from his curse, I want to run back and tell others how amazing His love truly is. I prayed that I could explain the circumstances and deception that led to my decision to have an abortion when I was faced with that choice up close and personally, and keep some of the girls from making the same choices someday. My hope was to even save them from putting themselves in a position that could lead to "having to" make that choice in the first place.

Every Choice Matters

It is vital for everyone to understand that while it may not be fair, it may not be politically correct, and it may not be comfortable to believe in personal responsibility and the reality that everything you do impacts not only yourself, but other people around you, it is true, nonetheless. <u>Every</u> choice you make affects others - without exception. Even something as silly as what kind of sandwich you have for lunch, not only affects your own body chemistry, but how much of that sandwich meat is left in the fridge or the restaurant for the next person who wants to order that kind of sandwich. The stakes and results of the impact vary, but the truth is this: every choice matters.

Proverbs 10:17 states, "He who heeds instruction is not only himself in the way of life, but also is a way of life for others. And he who neglects or refuses reproof not only himself goes astray but also causes to err and is a path toward ruin for others." This principle clearly states that our choices – good or bad, beneficial or detrimental – affect not only us, but those around us – including those we've never seen. Whether we like it or not, we are all interconnected and our choices can lift others from pits of depression and discouragement, or they can drop us and other people into degradation and futility, by what we say and what we do. The instruction and correction we avail ourselves of will affect our decisions. We need to heed instruction; we need to keep learning and let the things we learn increase our discernment and understanding and impact our decisions for the better in our immediate vicinity and in the world around us.

The person I was in my mid-teens was not "heeding instruction" and I was repeatedly "refusing and neglecting reproof" more often than not. If I did consider the possibility of unfavorable outcomes, I figured I would just deal with it later. I was overconfident in my ability to turn things to my favor. But I didn't see it that way at the time. I tended to point fingers of blame toward other people and situations I didn't like as the reason that I did and said things. As a result, I made poor decisions – both in action and in companionship.

Proverbs 27:17 says "Iron sharpens iron; so a man sharpens the countenance of his friend [to show rage or worthy purpose]." Make no mistake; our decisions *are* our own responsibility. We need to take ownership of the consequences of what we do. But our ability to stick to those decisions is often impacted by the people we associate with. The people we choose to be companions with can support us and encourage us to stay on the right course, or they can promote rebellion and turn us away from sound judgment. Instead of making choices of companionship, actions and goals that were in agreement with what I knew to be right, I chose what *felt* best, or gave the quickest, easiest solution to what I wanted at the time, irrespective of the future consequences.

Proverbs 12:26 shows us the application of this truth: "The righteous man is a guide to his neighbor, but the way of the wicked causes others to go astray". We need to decide the direction of our path in advance. Will we be companions of those who hold us to a right standard of moral character, or those who encourage us to do things and make choices that destroy our lives and the lives of those we love the most? Will we be an encouragement and "spur one another onto good deeds" (Hebrews 10:24)? Or will we be "a path of ruin"? We are clearly warned, "Do not be misled: 'Bad company corrupts

5

good character.'" (1 Corinthians 15:33). This was a lesson I learned the hard way, much later than I would have wanted to.

I'm not saying that *no one* tried to deter me from the self-destructive path I was on at the time, but there were plenty of other people who encouraged my rebellious attitudes, rewarded or condoned bad behavior and fed my self-pity that I "shouldn't have to go through" so many hard circumstances because of *other people's* choices. Those were the people I gravitated toward, the ones I listened to. The choices I made on my own as a result of this mindset were far more detrimental than anything *anyone else* had done to me! I was actively helping my worst enemy destroy my life.

That is the place I was in, physically, mentally, emotionally and spiritually back then. I was the oldest of five children, still reeling from my parents' divorce, deeply upset at the consequences I was living with because of other people's choices, although I wouldn't have been able to express it that way then. I was upset over having to take responsibility for things I had no control over. I wanted to start living so that the consequences I was living with were from *my own* choices and decisions. ("Be careful what you wish for – you might get it" fits too well here!)

I left home shortly after my 16th birthday, when the state's emancipation laws gave me more rights than I was ready for, and prevented my mother from forcing my return. This was only one in a chain of choices that brought me more pain than I could have imagined.

I continued going to school like nothing in the world was wrong. Moving in with my boyfriend who promised a ring and a wedding, I discovered less than a year later that I was expecting a baby. (It is a misnomer to call him my "boy-friend": he was seven years older than I was – a grown man with a full-time job, but it's easier to use that term.)

I was not aware that the "partner" I was with at that time was not willing to be a father. In my mind (and in "pillow talk" during more intimate moments) we had already decided that we were going to get married after I was done high school, and of course, to me, that meant having children. I was devastated to learn that his solution to my unexpected pregnancy was abortion, which he demanded on condition of my staying in his house. I was not ready for that kind of ultimatum and it scared and confused me.

My mother, newly divorced and still raising my three youngest siblings (the older of my younger brothers was no longer living at home), did not have the means to support two more. Our relationship was still pretty rocky and this was more than she could handle; she advised abortion as well.

My father advised against it, but he had no means of financially supporting us either if I chose to go through with the pregnancy and keep the baby. The only "crisis pregnancy" organization I knew about at the time was Planned Parenthood. The wording of the name sounded more noble than it was. Yes, they provided free (or less expensive) birth control, and with my limited means, that was important back then, but there was a dark side hidden from the much-publicized propaganda that I knew little about - yet.

I had not heard of BirthRight or CareNet or Operation Rescue or a host of other pro-life organizations that I know about now who offer a completely different set of choices I could have made and didn't – much to my dismay later in life.

During this whole process, I was living a double life. Hard-studying, parochial school girl during the day with concerns about grades, peer pressure, fitting in, growing up, (thank goodness the uniforms took care of the "what-to-wear" worries!) and at night I was the focus of a grown man's adult affections, "playing house" – fulfilling the role of a wife, without any of the commitment and documentation that would offer legal protections in case of traumatic life-events. There was no personal security beyond the emotions we both felt at the moment.

I hadn't realized any of that at the time. I just ignored the facts that I didn't want to see and rejected those who tried to point them out to me. I was having fun combining the school-girl thing during the day and wife-without-strings thing at night. It seemed for a while that I had the best of both worlds. But that was a lie. Living outside the boundaries for safety and godly living was taking more from me than I knew. Now it had led to choices I never wanted to make – and I didn't use the resources available at the time to make the right ones.

Deliberations

My thought processes at 16 were at best, severely jumbled, and I reasoned that I had to go through with the abortion for several reasons. I would not be allowed to continue living with the man who I was "pre-engaged" to, who told me he loved me and was going to marry me (I had a pre-engagement ring with a small diamond chip in it since the second week we were "dating", when I had given my virginity to him. He upgraded later to a bigger diamond in my junior year). My relationship with my mother was very contentious at that point and I didn't want to move back in with her. My father was living in a cold-water flat and could barely support himself at the time. I was the oldest of five. I knew the work that was involved in caring for a baby. Each time one of my brothers and sisters had been born, the crib went in my room. I knew up-close and personal about the 2 am feedings and being "up all night with a fever and then heading off to school". I had no illusions of that part of things.

People all around me were talking about not "ruining the rest of my life by limiting my options" so early, with "so much more of my youth to be lived" before I settled down. When adoption was posed as a possible alternative to abortion, I flat-out refused to consider it. I had heard about how many women so desperately wanted a baby and were unable to conceive for various reasons. I knew I was emotionally at a disadvantage to give a child as good a life as was possible with two parents who wanted and could give a stable and secure home for raising him or her. I reasoned – this is the thing that still makes me cringe as a justification for it all – if I went through with the pregnancy and gave the baby up for adoption so that he or she would have a pair of loving parents to care for them, "I would spend the rest of my life wondering where he or she was. What if I did find them and the adoptive parents wouldn't let me see him or her? I would be devastated. I couldn't bear that!"

I wish to God that I had gone the rest of the way through that thought – "I would rather kill my own child than to let someone else give him or her a happy, secure life". (As a side note, I should interject here that adoption is a much different proposition these days. Open adoption where the biological mom gets to choose or have some input as to who the adoptive parents are, have visitation, and a host of other options are available today that were never seriously considered before. Adoption is redemption in so many ways for all parties involved! I was not educated on the subject, so I was going by "what-if" fears instead of facts).

I can hope to believe that if I had followed that train of thought to its logical conclusion that I would have chosen differently back then, but I know from experience that I am capable of some pretty messed up choices in the panic and heat of the moment, and I will never know for sure.

That is one reason I am so humbled and grateful for God's grace and why I try not to be judgmental of other people when their choices seems so obviously harmful in hindsight. That is the true application of "There, but for the Grace of God, go I". We all need to develop the humility that comes from truly knowing that we too are capable of horrific decisions, given sufficient incentive. None of us can say what we would do in a certain situation, under all circumstances, especially that young in life with so few experiences and so little wisdom built up.

Young people don't have the wealth of life lived previously to be able to look back and compare past experiences with present circumstances and say – "Oh no! I am NOT doing that again! I remember what happened the last time this came up…" That is the real reason children need parents and older, godly counsel: to think through the consequences of thoughts in the deliberation stage and point out the flaws in hormone- and youth-compromised logic!

Often, people who have lived more of life, when asked for input while considering all the possible options, can see some of the outcomes of choices before we have to experience the pain of those consequences for ourselves. That is a major reason I believe in parental consent and notification – very often, what we fear in the middle of it all is far from the broader reality. And things we never considered, coming from a different perspective, could be the details we need to make well-informed choices. Older, wiser and sometimes cooler heads can bring clarity. My first child paid the ultimate price for my short-sighted, fear-induced, self-serving choices and my subsequent rejection of God's plan for life.

The day I went to the local Planned Parenthood clinic, the baby's father wouldn't come with me. He had to go to work. (He had taken time off before for amusement parks and dental cleanings, but he didn't want to come with me for this.) I didn't have my driver's license yet. A girlfriend and a mutual guy friend I knew through her brought me to the clinic and waited in the car for me. They were tearful about the situation, but enabled me to get there to maintain my living arrangements. Blinded by fear, and all the what-ifs of dread and doom, and not looking forward in hope to any of the good possibilities staying a mom right now might bring, I believed "I had no other choice".

I went in and had their pre-procedure chat with someone who was there. I don't know if she was a volunteer or an employee. While we were talking, she said something to the effect of it being "a lump of cells about this big". I sneered and said that I already knew that was a lie. She sat up a little straighter, leaned forward a little more and told me if I was having any doubts about this that I could stop and not go through with it. I was so upset about the whole thing that I didn't realize back then, I was being given a second chance to back out of the worst decision of my life.

I burst into tears and said "No, you don't understand! My boyfriend will throw me out if I don't do this!" I shut the tears off and determined that this was what I needed to do. (I was oblivious to how far along the baby's development had progressed in actuality, but I knew it wasn't just a bunch of random cells. I have thought many times in retrospect if only they had had an ultra-sound machine there for me to see…!)

I didn't feel like I had any other choice. Even that was a self-righteous perspective at the time. That was a lie. I had lots of choices! I had already made LOTS of them! In reality, as I look at it now, without a victim mentality, I had made decisions all along the way that put me in a position that required me to choose between life and death now. Ultimately, I was not willing to experience the possible outcomes of the other choices I had.

We All Fall Down

That is the reality of personal responsibility. It is a lot like a game of Jenga. Jenga is a party game where a tower is built by stacking layers of three rectangular blocks. By placing them one layer on top of another at opposing angles, you build it up until it stands 16 layers high. As each person takes their turn, one more block is removed, one-handed, from the lower levels of the tower without touching any other block, and then placed on top of the tower. Each block that is removed weakens the foundational structure, but the tower remains standing. When enough of the pieces are pulled out and balance is no longer possible, physics and gravity take over and the tower falls. The loser is the one who removes the final block, decreasing the stability of the tower to the point of its collapse.

Life choices are the same way. You may not get a bad result from one or two isolated bad decisions. You may be able to "counter-balance" or compensate for some of them along the way. But sooner or later, the continued pursuit of self-indulgence and ignoring consequences catches up with you. Habitual disregard for what is right over what feels good at the time leads to the destabilization of your life to the point of collapse and pain. (And the ironic thing is, it is possible to travel that destructive path feeling completely justified and self-righteous in your own choices, while pointing out and criticizing other people's shortcomings all along the way!)

The pain involved in the abortion procedure was worse than any period I had ever had – and that was saying quite a bit! I usually went through three days of being doubled over, with headaches and nausea that kept me home from school. This was way worse. I cried almost the whole time. I felt no relief; no one could make me feel better afterward. I laid down on a cot in a room with several other women, sipping orange juice and vomiting for more than an hour. During that time, I watched other women come in and go out of the same clinic. I was stunned by the ones who came in and practically danced out of the room afterward. No tears, no vomiting, and seemingly no adverse effects.

I actually found myself judging them for their lack of regret and distress! How could I have felt superior to them because I was taking it so bad and they weren't? We had just gone through the same procedure! How was I judging them when I had just allowed someone to kill my child for pay? I still don't know the answer to that one. In the midst of the worst choices of my life, I found something else to become self-righteous about!

When I got to the car, I was still crying and told my two friends how horrible it was. I wished I had never agreed to it, but it was too late. They helped me back to the apartment and after a little while, left me there to rest. When my boyfriend got back from work, we talked. I told him in graphic detail everything that had happened while I was there: the pain, the sounds, the thoughts running through my head, and all my regret. He held me and told me that if he had known how bad it was going to be, he would never have insisted that I go through with it.

We cried together and I stayed with him, still attending the catholic high school I was at, still living in my own misguided and ungodly choices – and believing him when he told me he loved me. I am certain he meant it (we are all broken, just in different ways). He was not an ogre. He had good qualities and had been my sole support through all this. We had good times, and a lot of fun with other activities. There were parts of all this that were very painful for him too. I was no saint, and had done and said things that hurt him deeply. But we had many differences on how we saw things and we hurt one another in the process. I knew this was not the best situation for either of us, but it was still easier than changing my path (for now).

The following year, still not changing the actions that got me pregnant in the first place, I became pregnant with our second child. I told my boyfriend I was "late", truly anticipating that this time we would get married and begin our family. I hadn't "done it on purpose"; I had been taking birth control pills for the whole time, even though they produced horrible migraine headaches. But it does say right on the flyers that come with them that they are not 100% effective. I was stunned when his answer was a short and to the point, "You know what to do".

I went from almost happily nervous to furious. "WHAT?! You told me the last time that 'if you only knew how horrible it was that you would never have insisted that I go through with it' and now you're telling me to do it again!?" I was right over the top – and fear was not anywhere near the picture. "You're right! I DO know what to do! I'm leaving!" and with a few obscene gestures causing white knuckles to be held high in the air, I started packing my stuff and getting out of "his" apartment.

I called the girlfriend who had taken me to Planned Parenthood the year before and told her what happened. She let me move in with her, trading babysitting services for room and board (She was in her mid-to-late twenties and had a two year old by this time and a full-time job). It must have been summer, because she lived out of town now and I was still high school age, but was not attending classes during these deliberations. We figured we would cross the appropriate bridges when we came to them, but I was determined not to have another abortion.

A few days (?) later, after the dust settled a little, I was getting scared again as to how I was going to be able to go through with all this. I looked at the pack of birth control pills I had been taking that had gotten thrown in with all my other things while I was packing. I wondered if I took one, would it "fix" the "problem"? I took one and went on with whatever I was doing at the time.

Later that night I cried and started to pray and apologize for what I had done. "God, I am so sorry! Please forgive me! I am scared and I shouldn't have done that. Please help the baby be healthy and help me figure out how to do this the right way!"
A couple days later I started to bleed – hard. I was so guilty. I felt so ashamed! I don't know if taking that one pill could have caused the miscarriage, but the torturous thoughts I've had over the years have *never* depended on facts. Recently, I was reassured that that kind of pill would not have been strong enough to cause a "spontaneous abortion". After all these years, it really is irrelevant. My intent at the time, no matter how momentary it was, was cause enough for decades of guilt and shame.

Don't get stuck in Semantics

In the current debate as to whether to call the "morning after" pills abortion pills or not, understand that what you call them is a moot point. Human hormone levels differ from one person to the next, and hormone supplements like birth control pills differ in strength and intensity. There are LOTS of them. Every person's body is different and therefore responds differently to medications and alterations in these hormones. There are too many variables in play to give absolute answers to questions that would apply equally to every person.

Because of these differences, pharmaceutical companies and doctors cannot say with certainty that their pills won't cause a miscarriage if taken by a pregnant woman – there is no way to make that claim with absolute veracity. With only one exception in all of history, the only way to prevent initiation of the cycle of life is to prevent sperm from contacting the egg. Once the sperm meets the egg, life has begun. (I just met someone the other day who asked a pivotal question: "if Life doesn't begin at conception, how does it GROW?" That pretty much lays it all on the table. Growth is not possible without life.)

All the physical characteristics that baby will have are wrapped up tightly in the DNA of that child and it is only a matter of time before we will be able to see what is already encoded in each of his or her developing cells. Whether the baby has started to develop and is prevented from implanting into the wall of the mother's uterus, or whether the baby is released from the uterus after implantation has already occurred, the effect is still the same: it is still abortion by pill. Period.

I went to the doctor's office crying and desperate for them to do something to save my baby. One of the doctors looked at me and impatiently said "What are you crying for? Everything is going to be fine". I half growled back, "Everything is NOT fine! I am losing my baby!" A pregnant 17-year-old staying with a friend, no job, was now miscarrying. I knew it wasn't the best situation to bring a baby into, but even in the uncertainty of my living arrangements – miscarriage or teen single mom – I didn't want to lose the life I was carrying. "Fine"? I guess it all depends on your point of view.

I lost my second baby. Depressed, remorseful, and grief-stricken over the loss, I was having a really hard time living inside my own head. But to be honest about it, I was also somewhat relieved. It was kind of like when a close relative dies after struggling with some debilitating disease – you are sad they are gone, but grateful they are not suffering any more – only in this context, the feelings' motives are way less noble, and mixed with all kinds of self-recrimination.

I was so completely self-absorbed and clueless that that is what it was! I was trying to sort out the guilt of the conflicting feelings I was having. I was a mess. I needed to "figure out what to do with my life". School was going to be starting up again and I needed to get there every day without a driver's license. When the baby's father found out that I had miscarried, he told me I could move back to his place. It was walking distance from school. I went back to him. (Can you say the word Stupid? I understand now that it all had to do with the emotional connection we had as a result of him being my first "love", the one I gave my virginity to. I understand he was the one I trusted with my provision and protection after I left home. Like the prodigal son, I was sure that life had to be better out there than dealing with my own broken family. I justified it all again. He wasn't all bad. He had good qualities. He could change. But seriously, how many times do I have to get burned before I stay away from the stove!?)

[Note: During the "40 Days" assembly, when I shared with the girls that I went back to him after all that, I saw looks of unbelief and disdain – good! I made the right point. I want to help other girls from making the same self-destructive choices now in their own lives. No other person on the planet is worth the kind of choices I made back then! But I was looking for comfort and stability without responsibility. It is ironic that I would choose to try to fill a "wife" role, but not want to retain the far-easier role of "daughter" and "sister" in my own family. The role I chose had far more responsibility than what I walked away from!]

Hard Lessons

I finished out my junior year at the same Catholic high school *and* I was now in wedding planning mode. In "negotiating" my return after the miscarriage, my boyfriend had given me an engagement ring with a bigger diamond in it and was now openly promising marriage immediately after graduation. I wasn't quiet about my living arrangements and showed off my new ring between classes and at afterschool activities. I was excited about the anticipated wedding - and getting closer to my senior year. I was looking forward to the white graduation gown, class ring and yearbooks – all the while thinking about wedding plans. I was even talking about having my boyfriend take me to the senior prom.

It's ironic that the thing I was looking most forward to was an intra-school tradition called being a "big sister". This is when a senior takes on an in-coming freshman as a "little sister", as someone to guide and show around the school, getting her comfortable with her new surroundings and mentoring her. I fondly remembered my own big sister from when I had been a freshman, a beautiful Philippine girl who sang incredibly well, and was the lead in all the school's annual musicals. She was my hero and a source of encouragement and stability in the messy first year of high school and my parents' divorce. I was looking forward to being that mentor now. And I saw nothing wrong with the dichotomy of that situation.

I was having my cake and eating it too, or so I thought. Some of the sisters at the school had several behind the scenes discussions that I knew nothing about concerning the influence a senior would have on underclassmen who saw a supposed role model "living in sin" and still being allowed to attend their school. The last day of my junior year, one of the sisters came up to me and told me I was not allowed to come back for my senior year. I was crushed and panicked. I vowed to move out of my boyfriend's house and "do it right". I would "move in with my dad". I "would do anything I needed to, to keep going to that school". I was openly begging them to let me stay. After all, I had endured all the underclassmen years and had kept my grades up, even after the divorce of my parents. Yes, I understood I was there on full scholarship, but "I had worked hard and *deserved* all the perks of being a senior at that school!" With everything else that had been going on in my life, that school had been more of an anchor of stability and normalcy than I knew, and I desperately needed it.

No one at the school had known about the abortion, or the miscarriage since it happened during the summer. They weren't using that as an argument for my leaving, and I obviously didn't bring it up. I had thrown myself whole heartedly into everything good at the school. I had been excitedly involved in the musicals, helped with anything I could – cleaning classrooms with the sisters after the school year ended, doing concerts with the choir at a nearby women's prison for Christmas. I didn't want to give all that up! A saddened face tried to explain to me: "Tracy, you've had two years to change your ways. Sometimes the choices we make close doors that we can't open, even if we begin to do things the right way." That was one of the doors.

I flipped out, switching from deep sadness and pleading with them to change their minds, vowing changes I truly believed I would make given the fork in the road I now faced, to yelling angrily that they were out of touch and clueless about "real life". I decided *they* were the ones who had the problem and I took on a self-righteous attitude (again). I was the biggest loser through the choices I made and refused to recant all through my underclassman years. Now when I was faced with the loss of so many milestones I had so dearly looked forward to: Prom, the class trip, the regal graduation in the new auditorium, and so on, it was easier to blame it on others' "antiquated religious beliefs", than to take responsibility for the consequences of my self-destructive and self-deluded choices and accept the blame myself for my own pain.

I defiantly made arrangements for night school and got the one remaining credit I needed for history and my fourth year of English. I graduated in December – six months earlier than my classmates – through local adult education. Taking a "licking my wounds" attitude and consoling myself with early graduation, I now had my day time free from class schedules. Routine and daily expectations were gone, making it harder to feel any purpose for my days.

And I still stayed on that broken path that made my heart bleed! I reasoned that if I wasn't going to be able to go to the school anyway, why should I move in with my dad? I stayed in the house with my boyfriend for another year. It was easier to get angry at someone else than it was to accept responsibility that my own actions had caused the current situation.

Several years later, while visiting the school and talking with one of the other sisters about the events of that year, she told me I could have appealed the decision. But it was too late. It was already done. And that lesson was one hard-learned truth I have carried forward to other things in my life. It was painful to learn, but looking back on it now, it was a turning point I needed to understand to be free of the behavioral rut I was in.

True Love

Those who love us – truly love us – will sometimes need to make choices to teach us and enforce those hard consequences when we are younger. When we fight against their correction, their steadfastness in discipline attests loudly that their main concern is for our growth and ultimate good character, even when it feels like doing so will rip their hearts out in the face of our desperate tears or angry, hurtful words. I wouldn't see it at the time, but these sisters, the nuns who were trying to teach me the right path to follow, loved me far more than I knew. In staying with my boyfriend, I thought I was choosing love over religious intolerance. I was wrong. I was choosing my own lust and others' acceptance of my wrong choices over true Love and concern for my welfare. I have since experienced times when I have been the one who tearfully enforced consequences I did not want to stick by; it is a hard position to be in. I am very grateful for their decision today.

The longer we wait to learn (and later offer) that kind of love in enforcing those painful lessons, the more painful the lesson has to be to get the same message across to our ever-thickening hearts and heads. Some people never have someone love them so tenderly and deeply to take the pain on themselves for the lessons we must learn. Sound familiar? Parents all over the world have said, "This hurts me more than it hurts you." As kids we never believe that, but when we become parents, we feel it personally. Parents feel pain over some of their children's choices; just like our Heavenly Father feels pain when we make choices against His instructions for safety and good living.

That, in its essence, is the difference between human love and God's love for us – human love can be a gushy feeling that ebbs and flows and passes based on circumstances, but God's Love is a *decision* He makes in His Perfectness. Agape Love: to do and say the right things for the ultimate good of the other person no matter what the personal cost to the 'Lover' along the way. *That's* how God loves *us*.

Chris Rice sings a song that says in part: "Sometimes Love has to drive a nail into Its Own hand". Jesus did that. Jesus took the pain on Himself to offer the Way out of no-choice-but-death, to offer us life. He is accused of intolerance, of exclusivity, of being out-dated and hopelessly out-of-touch. Nothing could be further from the Truth! He took the pain to give me and you opportunities to learn lessons from *temporary* consequences to save us from the permanent one – hell.

I was so blessed at the time to have someone so in touch with Jesus -the Ultimate Lover of my Soul - to be willing to take the pain of the hurtful words and blinding tears of my rage when I didn't get my way back then, to teach me this lesson – even though it would be many years before I realized that was what it was at the time! Sometimes WE close doors through our own choices that we would rather have remained open. We choose. And choose. And choose again. Then we get the consequences of those choices. It is not to be blamed on others.

Acknowledging that fact is the beginning of growth and real change in us. We need to choose differently. Repeatedly. And *then* we get the *good* consequences - rewards - for our self-discipline and wise, but sometimes painful decisions. I am truly fortunate to have had people in my life who loved me like that. My prayer now is that I can love others in the same way — even if it hurts (and is misunderstood) for now. This lesson has stayed with me like a jewel - and has gained many more facets of realization to reflect beauty through the painful cuts of my life. But I wasn't ready to admit anything yet — I needed more consequences to steer me right...

Another Wake-up Call

Shortly after I completed adult ed., I turned 18 and decided college was the next step in my intention to "better myself" and contribute to my own support instead of being solely dependent on others for the things I needed. The disappointment I felt over not being able to finish high school with my other classmates, now coupled with broken promises of a wedding. I had pressed my fiancé for a wedding date; pointing to the engagement ring he had given me as proof that had been our joint intention all along and crying over the proper graduation I had "given up for him". He said it was "just a ring" and he wasn't ready for marriage. I felt used. Because of my involvement with this man, I had lost the whole teen high school experience of graduation year and everything that goes with it. Now the wedding I had chosen over those rights of passage in my life was all a lie. I felt betrayed. Now, amid all the other things that were happening in my life, things took another dramatic turn in my living arrangements.

I moved in with my dad in the cold-water flat and tried to stay away from my ex-fiancé, fighting against all the previous feelings I had for him. I "see-sawed" back and forth for a while, "dating" other guys and alternately trying to make up with him. It was an emotional roller-coaster. But I had begun to see more options open up for life in general.

The college I attended was a local community college that allowed me to live at home and still take courses during the day without all that expensive "campus living" - dealing with dorms and meal plans, and so on. I worked hard, got involved with some very colorful people in the drama club and school newspaper. They were wonderful, supportive and lived in some pretty unconventional ways.

It was not anything like I had been acquainted with in a Catholic high school and small mill town setting where I lived. I made life-long friends there–but my moral standing tanked even farther. I still had some standards, but little by little surrendered more of what I should have been defending. Even if I was not willing to do things myself, I reasoned back then that I "had no right to judge others" for what I knew to be wrong. Tolerance was the watch-word and personal moral standards were thought to be an "uneducated" perspective needing enlightenment.

As an adult, I now know the difference between judgment and discernment. I still love the people I met in college. A couple of them helped me through some of the darkest days of my life. I still get to see some of them. They are dear to my heart and I miss seeing the ones I've lost contact with. I have fond memories of the time we spent together, even though some of the situations we put ourselves in hurt each of us in different ways. In retrospect, I've learned so much more about how God sees us. I now understand that He loves us so deeply, we simply can't fathom it. God has compassion for our pain and the broken places in our hearts, as He enforces the consequences that will steer us right.

I understand now that He wants nothing in this world more than being given the chance to heal us. But He abides by our choices in that area too. He sends people into our lives to guide us, He works in our hearts, softening our rough edges and breaking off pieces of the hardened shells we build around our hurts. He pokes and prompts us with His voice of conscience and sometimes knocks us off our horses to get our attention. We have to choose, but He is not a distant bystander in the process. If we truly want to experience life the way we are meant to, we need to accept God's perspective and let Him show us His safety zones for living our lives under His protection.

It's not about condemnation and rejection of people. It's about deciding to do what you know is right, avoiding wrong actions, even if they "feel good" at the time, and living accordingly. Judging people and passing sentence on them is wrong, but discerning between right and wrong actions, and making decisions based on sound moral principles is critical to having a life worth living!

I took chances and put myself in positions that make me shudder when I think about all of the adverse possibilities. I repeatedly avoided accountability for my own choices. And as a first-born girl with an over-developed sense of responsibility, that was extremely hard to do! I was always at war with my conscience. I was trying to get connection and acceptance in other relationships. I did not like the direction these new experiences were taking my life in and the changes I saw in who I was becoming. It scared me. I was manipulative, angry, and lied to get my way. I was cynical most of the time and missed the easy laughter my loss of innocence had taken from me. I started to keep different company and make more choices I could live with. It was a start in the right direction.

When I think what could have happened if God had not protected me from myself back then, it still simultaneously brings mixed feelings of deep regret and intense gratitude. I was still acting like I was in the driver's seat. I was not. I am supremely grateful that "a man's mind plans his way, but the Lord directs his steps and makes them sure." (Proverbs 16:9)

Even in the sorry state I was in, God was working in my heart and directing me in the way He wanted me to go. Make no mistake: there are still consequences for my actions that I am keenly aware that still affect my life today, all these years later. But redemption and Grace are powerful allies and Jesus is faithfully stubborn in His tenacity and persistence to keep what is His!

New Beginning

I had met the man who is now my husband while I was living with my boyfriend, the summer I turned 16. He was good friends with someone else we both knew and we talked intermittently on the rare occasions we saw one another during my last two years in high school while all this turmoil was happening. He didn't know about what was going on with me because our conversations were mostly weather-related and what local events or parties we had gone to. ☺ I knew his mother from the town hall, and whenever I would see her, I would ask her to tell Steve I said "hi!" but that's as far as it went up to that point.

One night, while I was still trying to "ride the reconciliation rollercoaster" with my ex-fiancé, we decided it would help rekindle our relationship by going to a local Knights of Columbus fund-raiser dance in our community. Maybe some dancing and loud music would help. Things were not going well between us that night. There was no "rekindling", just icy walls and hurt feelings. I saw Steve when we walked in and we started talking. We considered each other friends, but hadn't seen one another for a long time and wanted to "catch up". My date decided it was more than that and got ticked off. Steve tried to smooth out the situation. Nope. (You know how women have the reputation for "shutting off" their partners when they're upset about something? My date decided not dancing was in order for my "indiscretion"). It was finally obvious to me this was going nowhere.

I decided to make the best of the surroundings by continuing my conversation with Steve. We talked about all kinds of things, but kept the conversation light and friendly. He was funny and interesting. He was into hiking, hang gliding and was taking flying lessons. He had a full-time job building submarines in a shipyard and was an avid reader. When my date refused to dance, and I had resorted to moving around in my chair to the music, Steve asked me if I would dance with him. Of course! (but only the fast dances. I was, after all, there with someone else.) Steve's mom and dad were both there too, along with most of the other people we knew in town. We wanted to make sure everything was above board; it stayed just dancing and chit-chat.

He was hesitant to ask me out. I was clueless that he wanted to. I was still with the other guy, but our conversation (and my date's reaction to it), helped me to finally realize a few things. The possessiveness without commitment, the repeated refusals for marriage accompanied by all the "benefits" of that arrangement, jealousy over any conversations with others, all came to a head. I decided (again) to try to do things right. A week later, I moved back in with my dad. Steve and I began dating very shortly after. It was four months before my 19th birthday.

I wanted to live right. But old habits die hard and right ways of thinking take time without encouragement and support. In truth, within four months Steve and I were living together. We justified it by pointing to my dad's apartment and complaining about its size and facilities. We were in love. We really didn't need an excuse.

Most of the people around us were of the same mind-set we were – some people call it situational ethics. Sure, it's wrong, but you have good reasons for what you're doing. Either way, most people were not telling us that cohabitation was wrong, even though we knew it from our upbringing. It was socially acceptable. Anyone who used the term "living in sin" was marginalized and ignored. We had our own plan. We would get married after I graduated college in two years. We minimized anything that opposed that decision. In the meantime we got to know one another, we went to family functions on both sides of the family – preferring his because of my rocky relationship with my mother, but never hesitating to take my younger brothers and sisters out for day trips or vacations to Vermont and such.

Steve knew about my abortion and miscarriage. We used birth control pills to "prevent untimely reoccurrences". (Why I would trust their effectiveness after all this I don't know - and I was still getting migraines.) I am so glad that God is patient and gracious. We both knew His standard of marriage before living together and having sex, but disregarded it as "old-fashioned". We both knew some of what results from ignoring that standard we were both currently living with. We justified it and ignored God in our relationship. He just wasn't part of our lives at that point – or so we thought. God still loved us. God still protected us from some of the horrible consequences that some other people have had to deal with. I can't explain the Grace that we were benefiting from, and taking for granted the whole time. But God was still working in our hearts little by little, drawing us closer to Him - and we were changing.

My relationship with Steve was very different than the one I had previously. I was grateful for his unselfish care and concern for me. He was, and continues to be, a man of character and sacrificial protection and provision for me, even in the face of some hefty obstacles. No relationship is perfect, but he is my hero in a lot of ways, and that has deepened over the years of our lives together.

When I did get pregnant a year later, there was no doubt we would keep the baby. We were nervous, but looking forward to it. When I started bleeding and lost my third child, I was heart-broken. Steve consoled me while I shuddered with tears, fearing it was "all my fault" and that somehow my body was damaged after two D & C's (one for the abortion and one done after the "pill-induced" miscarriage to "prevent infection"). Now I feared I would lose every baby I carried. After all, I had already lost two of my children following the abortion. Would this continue forever?

The doctors assured me that there was no residual damage from the abortion (of course), and we sought "genetic counseling" – blood tests to see if there was a chromosomal or other genetic reason for my body not to carry full-term. Negative. Nothing there. (I would find out much later that I had severe endometriosis – my uterus was "fractured" and pieces of it eventually began growing and attaching themselves to other organs in my body. This condition caused extreme pain every month that no over-the-counter pill could touch for relief. It made it a lot harder for my body to carry my babies. I had no idea that endometriosis could adversely affect a pregnancy, but felt the painful effects of this truth nonetheless. No one knows whether this condition was initiated or aggravated by the abortion procedure, as we had no "before" picture or baseline to go by, but we do know it got worse over time.)

We comforted one another with the idea that we just weren't emotionally or financially ready to begin our family yet and I focused on finishing college. (It is strange sometimes what we tell ourselves in times of disappointment and self-consolation was "not meant to be"!)

Truth Hurts Before It Sets You Free

Steve and I were married two weeks after my college graduation in 1984. During this time, we watched lots of science programs on TV and came upon the public TV program Nova. We watched it all the time. When watching "The Miracle of Life" episode and seeing a fiber optic camera's view of babies' growth from conception through birth, I was hammered with guilt.

The program documents each milestone, each stage of development with the technology available at that time, showing when the heart starts beating (two weeks in utero! Before you even know you're "late"), when the arm buds have finger bones visible through translucent skin, when the eyelids form, and so on, right up to the day the baby is born.

I wanted to see it. I wanted to know. Something that should have been just an awe-inspiring wonder was intensely painful. I started doing the math – three and a half to four months along - everything was already formed! An ultrasound would even have been able to tell me whether it was a boy or a girl at that point! Basically, the only things still left to develop on my first baby at the time of the abortion were hair, lungs and fingerprints – and doubling in size.

My husband held me and comforted me while my soul was racked with grief and guilt. I was nearly hysterical, rocking back and forth sobbing over the undeniable evidence of what really happened years earlier. I didn't want to miss seeing the program, but it brought fresh heartache to the grief of my two miscarriages and compounded the guilt over my decision to abort. People tried to be helpful, telling me time would lessen my pain over this loss. That was not what I was experiencing at all!

[Note: In several of Jimmy Evans' teachings from Marriage Today (www.marriagetoday.com), he relates the differences in physical healing and emotional healing. He points out the old cliché "time heals all wounds" may be valid for physical injury, but not for our souls. Because our bodies are created with built-in repair systems like white blood cells, a lymphatic system, a digestive tract, renal system and lungs, it can attack disease, collect and eliminate bodily waste and get it out of the way. Our physical bodies, given time and rest, will heal. "Emotional and mental wounds don't heal like physical wounds. In the case of physical wounds, there is an immediate attempt by the body to heal itself. After a period of time, we are healed "naturally". However, our inner wounds aren't that way. The scars of our soul don't heal until we have allowed them to."[1]

Our emotional selves do not have the "automatic" immunity and healing systems in place. Attributing emotional healing to time itself is futile expectation. In our bodies, healing is a result of Divine processes in bodily engineering. A different method of healing was designed for our souls.

When we are emotionally damaged, time is our enemy. Time makes emotional wounds fester and breed bitterness and twists our perceptions in other areas, in essence, "spreading the infection". In our emotions, there is no "built in" system for anything but self-defense mechanisms that put things in storage until we can deal with it later. Denial, transference, repression, and distraction are all ways our minds use as coping mechanisms to dissipate emotional pain.

In the beginning these coping mechanisms can be a beneficial buffer until we are in a safe enough place to deal with these painful memories. But if we don't take the time to face these wounds and clean them out with Truth and Grace, the pain magnifies and waits just under the surface, like a time bomb that can go off at the strangest times and triggered by the least expected incidents. It will not be ignored indefinitely. And when it finally rears its ugly head, it can be unbelievably crippling. I was discovering this the hard way.]

From the time I was 16, through everything that was happening to this point; I couldn't look at another baby without crying. When I would be out in public and see a mother holding an infant I would ache inside and turn away. If it was someone I knew who offered to let me hold him or her, it was intensely painful. Sometimes I could hold my emotions together and be polite, and even enjoy it for a little while. I would let them know how happy I was for them and look into their little faces. Sometimes I could hold them without losing it right away, but when I was alone later, I would be so self-condemned and grief-stricken I didn't want to be in the same room with myself! This went on for years – sometimes more intense than others. Some of you know EXACTLY what I am talking about.

I was, and am, so grateful for my husband! He was always comforting and supportive, even while he was going through his own grief. He was part of my healing. A model of what a man is supposed to be for his wife in so many ways! And even though I did not recognize it at the time, God's love and comfort was balming the wound until I got to the place where I could relinquish it to Him for complete healing!

My self-condemnation was relentless. And it was doing more

damage than I knew. It was actually keeping me from the relief I so desperately needed. I was so legalistic in my own life and had seen that character flaw in so many of the adult men in my life, that it became how I saw God too – a stern, demanding, punisher instead of an open-armed, something-special-for-My-little-girl, wipe-your-tears-on My-shoulder kind of God that He really is for His children. (I guess for me that was the difference between a father and a grandfather – the difference between conditional and unconditional love – my dad's affection seemed to be based on what I did or didn't do; I knew both my Grandpa and my Pepiere loved me regardless). I didn't view God that way up to this time and it affected how I did most everything.

Steve and I waited over a year before *planning* our next baby. At this point, I had made an inner vow that I would make sure my children all knew they were planned and would have no chance at all to believe, like I had, that they were "accidents".

When I discovered I was pregnant again, I was thrilled and hopeful. When we had gone three months into this pregnancy, I started bleeding again. I begged and pleaded with God to save my baby. I didn't want Him to "punish me for my abortion by taking away another one". People I talked to before this had told me "God doesn't work that way". I pointed to David and Bathsheba's first child and used it as proof that "yes, He could (2 Samuel 11-12)!" I didn't want false comfort. I didn't want to feel condemned. I didn't want to lose my baby because I had messed up so badly earlier in my life. I prayed for the thousandth time for God to forgive me for what I had done and please let this one live. I still had (and have) so much to learn about the love of God. He met me where I was at the time. He always does. The bleeding stopped a couple days later.

My daughter was born in October, healthy, complete, and with a full head of hair. We love her dearly to this day and are grateful that God doesn't depend on our misconceptions of Who He is for how He responds to us as we grow in our very limited understanding of Him. He is love. He is tender and caring toward His children. Sometimes we go through hard things. There are consequences to our own choices. But He "never leaves us nor forsakes us. " (Hebrews 13:5)

A few months later, enjoying every breath, every day of her life, we found out we were expecting again. A couple other cousins and friends were pregnant at the same time. We were all thrilled. I miscarried again.

This time was bad. I was four months along, and knew exactly how developed everything was. I passed out in the examination room waiting for someone to come in. There was no call cord or button in the room and I was hemorrhaging. My husband yelled for help and I came to with an IV being jammed into the back of my hand. I had lost another baby. This time was a little easier to deal with the loss. I had my little girl at home who needed me to care for her, and it helped distract me through some of my grief. It also helped both of us to bond closer to one another.

A few days later, after my husband had gone back to work, I went out for the mail. Not thinking anything of it, I opened a card addressed to both of us. It was all white with swirling script letters sending condolences on our loss. I burst into tears and threw the card across the room like it was on fire. I didn't even know who signed it. All kinds of things were running through my head. Who would do something like that?

I pointed to it from across the room when Steve got home

from work. He had no idea what was wrong. He picked it up and read it and his face softened as he tried to explain. It was a heart-felt expression of sympathy from a dear older man that Steve worked with and his wife. As Steve held me in the kitchen, tears pouring down my face again, he began *apologizing* for the guy: "Tracy, if he had any idea you would react this way, I am sure he would never have sent the card. He was trying to let us know they felt bad for us." I felt better about it then. It hadn't been some cruel joke. It was a tender acknowledgment of our loss. Only then was I able to accept the true intention the card was sent with. I hadn't intended to be so cynical about it; it just hit me so far out of left field! I had never thought about sending anyone a card for a miscarriage before. Didn't most people just put it behind them and go on?

I have no idea what their personal story was concerning children and any possibility of their having dealt with this situation themselves in the past, but they will always be remembered fondly for stepping out and making that effort to reach out to me in the middle of that emotional black hole I was in then.

Over the next few weeks, friends and relatives started coming out of the woodwork to tell us about their own losses. You don't know how many other people miscarry, or how many times - even in your own family - until something like this happens. There was unspoken comfort in the hugs I got from women who knew the depth of my pain, without me having to say a word.

My husband didn't want to try again. He didn't want to risk losing me and having our little girl grow up without her mom. That never even occurred to me. I took a different tack. I consoled myself in the loss with the determination that in four more months... (did I mention I was stubborn?) We waited the required time after the miscarriage and I told Steve I wanted to try one more time. We did. The "usual" first trimester spotting terrified us, but again cleared after several days.

Our son was born one month prematurely in October on my husband's father's birthday. (He had died six months after that dance I told you about earlier.) We named our son after his dad. The fact that he had 4 more weeks to go meant he had some additional hurdles to cross. We went through a week of additional medical intervention due to jaundice.

A lot of prayer and time in the children's ward stabilized him so we could bring him home permanently. We were done. We had two beautiful children - a boy and a girl, both healthy and both doing well. We decided we were not going to go through those risks again.

A New Perspective

Throughout all these years, I was still beating myself up over the horrible choices I made and the pain they caused a lot of people besides me. God has revealed several key points that helped me change my heart and mind toward His character and my faith. God told me in Psalm 139 that His "thoughts toward us are precious" and "vast are the sum of them" (v. 17).

That was a completely foreign concept to me. I really hadn't thought that God particularly cared or thought about me really, unless I was begging Him to save me from something, then didn't He just back up again, like the song, watching me from a distance?

On the contrary, He says in Jeremiah 1:5 "Before I formed you in the womb, I knew you and approved of you."Not only did God make me Himself inside my mother's body (as He does with each child everywhere in the world), He *knows* everything about me and *loves* me and *approves* of me! Just like He does for you.

He may not be thrilled with some of the things I do – in fact, I know some of my actions hurt Him deeply – but I know now He never stops loving me and approves of me as His little girl. That is a huge gift to my wounded soul!

He tells us in Lamentations chapter 3 that even when we *feel* like He has abandoned us and we *feel* lower than ashes, "God's mercies are new every morning" and "His compassions never fail" (v. 22-23). Every morning, every day, He gives us a clean slate to work with. Yes, we need to confess our sins and repent from the wrong we've done, but He's not sitting there with an ever-increasing list of things we have to make up for and dig ourselves out from under before He will consent to help us when we call out to Him. He rises quickly to show us mercy and come to our aid. (Have you read the Psalms?)

He's completely aware of our limitations. He says "He remembers that we are dust" (Psalm 103:14) and He "knows the heart of man" (John 2:24). He knows we aren't perfect, not even close! He knows we are capable of some pretty hurtful and outright horrible things. But He also knows how hard we try sometimes to get it right and He meets us wherever we are when we turn to Him for help.

As I took this all in, certain facts began to emerge and set me free. Even though God is the Ultimate Father, He is very different from our earthly dads in some very important ways. Check out Hebrews chapter 12. Yes, He disciplines us. But not like our human dads. Our parents have their own baggage; their own fears, damage and issues. God has none of those hindrances in His relationship with us. He doesn't have a temper tantrum and hit us out of a lack of self-control. Or guilt. Or embarrassment. He trains us "for our certain good" (v. 10), in ways that He can see far in advance that will allow us to grow up to be the people He created us to be.

Do you remember your mom's secret weapon as you got older? "I'm not angry with you – I'm just disappointed." Remember how bad that made you feel? In a way, at least for a short time, it worked as an internal motivator. It worked with even more effectiveness and less effort than the physical, external threats after a while.

But God doesn't even go there with us. He <u>can't</u> be disappointed in us. He KNOWS what we are going to do before we are faced with any situation. He gives us choices. He tells us some of the consequences ahead of time. He even tells us what choices He wants us to make. He blesses us with so many beautiful and beneficial experiences along the way to encourage us. He grieves over some of our choices, to be sure. But He lets us make those choices, after giving us direction and multiplied opportunities to choose well.

When we choose otherwise, He shows us our error and leads us to repentance. He *does* let pain happen to teach us to avoid certain things (2 Cor. 7:10). And He reaches out to restore us and redirect us when we turn to Him after the fall. He draws us to Him for what we need and offers Himself to us with open hands every time. He keeps knocking at the doors of our hearts. Sometimes He uses blessings and sometimes He uses hardships, to motivate and empower us. But He always reaches out in Grace for our every need – if we only have eyes to see it!

There are so many places in the Bible that He corrected my understanding of His character and His heart toward me. He closed the gap between us in great love and lifted me out of so many pits and problems – a lot of them of my own making – that I have long ago lost track. I have learned more about His heart than I knew back then. I still have a long way to go – and I am looking forward to the journey – to the adventures He has in store for the process.

***

I tried to fit in everything I could when I shared most of my story with the girls and the sisters who were in the room that day, whatever I could fit into a 45 minute time slot. I told them I understand now how God warns us in Romans 1:21 that our "senseless minds are darkened" and we "become futile in our thinking" when we don't follow His way of living. I was insistent upon making choices that I knew were opposed to His path, and it began "to seem right to me" (Prov. 14:12) as I heaped up friends and other people around me that "satisfied my own liking and fostered the errors I held" (2 Tim 4:3). I shared the pain and rejection I felt, as well as part of the healing that God gave me by repeating to my guilt-ridden heart: "There is now therefore no condemnation for those who are in Christ Jesus" (Romans 8:1). And how He and I got together to rebuild me as a new vessel - "reshaping my clay" (Jeremiah 18:1-6) for His purpose.

I could use my past as a warning and an encouragement to others. The mess I made could be redeemed to be a message of hope. The test I had failed could become a testimony and beacon of truth to keep other girls on the path I had repeatedly strayed from. It was not a single choice. It was a series of decisions that put me in places I should never have been. I didn't have to experience those heart-breaking situations, but now that I had, Jesus could use them to bring trustworthy and experienced advice to other generations, one life or one group at a time.

A Series of Choices

Long before I decided to abort my baby, I had complete control over my previous choices. I nursed resentful thoughts of being cheated of a "normal" childhood with the added responsibilities of being part of a larger family. I thought if I was "on my own", I would make better choices, have more money, and be less restricted. I was not "on my own". I was allowing my thoughts to be influenced by a darker plan, a plan for destruction and pain. That is why we are told to "take every thought captive and make it obedient to Christ" (2 Cor. 10:5) and warned that the "enemy comes only to kill, steal and destroy" (John 10:10). THAT is why Christian fellowship and a shared community of faith is so critical in our lives. THAT is why we are told to "confess our sins one to another – so that we may be healed"! (James 5:16). It is when we bounce ideas off of one another with the Bible as the guidebook, adhering to our intention of allowing God to direct us toward His path in concert with other believers that we keep one another from destruction and deception. THAT is "iron sharpening iron"! (Proverbs 27:17)

Some things that happen to us are not our fault. Sometimes other people's choices impact us in horrible ways and we are damaged in the process. It is never a girl's fault if someone forces themselves on her. That is a violent choice of someone else and has nothing to do with love or even sex – it's a power play, and is always wrong. You didn't ask for it. You didn't invite it. It was not your choice that caused it to happen. If you are fore-warned and personal security conscious, you can make choices before an incident happens that can determine where you are and who you are with. This may not eliminate the possibility of difficult situations arising, but some choices you make do give you the ability to minimize circumstances leading to detrimental outcomes. Here are a few of them:

Don't wear revealing clothing. It is your choice what you wear. If you're advertising things you should be keeping covered, others who hide their true intent will get the wrong ideas about your character. You can be stylin' and wear clothes that make you look good without revealing your body. Even bathing suits can be cute *and* modest. You can have respect for yourself. You have immense value as a person, no matter what your family, economic or social standing. You are a daughter of God Himself! Don't dismiss that value to give someone a cheap thrill or get some superficial attention — you're worth more than that.

I'm not saying you have to dress like a Pilgrim. Appreciating you have a nice shape is not wrong, but wearing short-cut or see-through t-shirts that show your bra, or super-short hot pants, is going to attract people who "lust" after you, not value you. There is a difference. Seeing yourself respectfully and dressing in modest style — whatever style you choose to express yourself in - will foster the appreciation of others based on your character and help deter those who would treat you with disrespect due to false assumptions based on your revealing attire.

You don't have to date so early! Society markets lots of things using sex and physical intimacy to target age groups that should still be learning to navigate the world around them. You should be learning about the beauty of nature, the intricacies and interdependence of life in science class, and how to apply what you're learning in the classroom to the real world. Don't be tricked into thinking you're missing something if you're not in a serious physical relationship yet. It's foolish to commit your life or your body to someone when you know so little about what path your life will take from here! Hang out with a *group* of friends – there is no need to "pair off". Find out how the world works, how friendships and common interests build firm interpersonal foundations *way* before marriage and physical intimacy throw more lessons your way!

Group activities give lots of socialization opportunities without you being alone with anyone. Have fun! Enjoy working toward a purpose. Help others. Get involved in community projects. Get in a good youth group– if you don't have one, get a couple of trusted adults or a pastor to start one! Help one another be accountable for good stuff! Find out what your talents and gifts are and take the time to develop them. There is so much about you that you don't know yet!

That doesn't mean you cannot have friends of the opposite sex. Different perspectives on life are a great growing opportunity. Just understand that avoiding situations that promote a physical relationship with someone when you're still in your early teens is in *your own* best interest. There is plenty of time for that stuff later.

Just because it feels good (for now) doesn't mean it's right. Physical intimacy feels good at the time because it's supposed to – it was *designed* to feel good. If it didn't feel good the human race would not have continued to reproduce! Don't let that get in the way of you understanding a critical fact: there is a right time and right place for that kind of pleasure – and now ain't it! There is a term for having sex before marriage. God calls it fornication and in dozens of places, He clearly says it's wrong – *and He tells us why* (Mark 7:21, Acts 15:29, 1 Cor. 6:15-20, 1 Cor. 10:8 & 11, 2 Cor. 12:21,Gal. 5:19, Eph. 5:3, Col. 3:5, 1 Thes.. 4:3 ...see what I mean?).

God created sex. It's not something the devil came up with to give us some fun on the side because being good is so boring! God made it feel good. But satan, (which means the adversary, also called the deceiver, accuser, and father of lies!), twists that too and says, "God is keeping something good from you with all His rules". He tells us, "What the heck, if it feels good, do it!" without restriction, without safety, knowing the damage we will bring on ourselves. What he doesn't tell you, and what God does point out to us in His Word ahead of time, is *sin is pleasurable – for a time,* but in the end, it leads to death. (Heb 12:25, Ps 16:25) When we live only for the moment, we miss out on those warnings. Then, our painful results give satan the joy of gloating over, and enjoying our pain when we fall into the shame and regret as things ultimately go sour. The Bible does warn us that "the wages of sin is death" (Rom 6:23). I submit to you that we lose more than our innocence or our physical life. We incur the death of opportunity, death of joy, death of satisfaction with life itself (always searching and never finding true satisfaction) – and death of a healthy, whole body.

Syphilis, gonorrhea, herpes, AIDS, Chlamydia and other "communicables" became so wide-spread because people thought more of the here and now pleasure than the safety of godly choices. They relinquished their self-control when things got more intimate than was appropriate for the time. And millions of people are paying the price for those kinds of choices every day. Be smarter than that. Knowing those things are out there looking for another host – and that some of them will kill you - should give you sufficient reason for restraint. Be realistic in your expectations of your own appetites and keep yourself from getting hot and bothered in the first place. Don't think you can start off and then trust yourself to stop "before it gets too far" – it doesn't work that way. Listen to the warning – it could save your life!

What's the reward for keeping yourself sexually pure until after you're married and sticking with that one person forever? Why wait? Because God knows what He's talkin' about and He makes it worth your while! Ever hear the song by Blue Country, "Good Little Girls"? If *both of you* wait until the wedding night – ooh la la! Without the shame and guilt of previous heartbreak, without the possibility of diseases cutting in on the fun, without looking to twisted variations for satisfaction – you are completely free to enjoy every moment of exploring each other and having more fun with it than you can possibly imagine – when it's the *right* time! Don't settle for lust - Love waits.

Alcohol is a major contributor to releasing inhibitions. So are drugs. Don't allow yourself to be taken advantage of because of your decreased self-control under the influence. Any honest person will tell you the decisions they made while under the influence are not the ones they would have made if they'd been sober. Learn this by accepting the truth of it instead of by experience – it's a lot less painful that way.

Your Parents are truly not your enemy. It is natural for us to have differences with our parents when we are growing up and adolescence is hard on all of us. But understanding that in most cases, our parents really do want what is best for us can sideline a lot of additional misunderstanding. Some of their angst is due to the simple truth that they've been through a lot of the experiences your facing and they are concerned for you - knowing the things they did in those same situations when they were younger! Realize your parents can undoubtedly save you a pretty fair amount of pain from these same experiences - if you listen to their advice. They may be fairly new at the "parent" thing, but they've already been teenagers! You may find you can maximize the good aspects of that old adage "The apple doesn't fall very far from the tree" and benefit from their footsteps. Cut them a little slack and remember they know more than they've told you about so far, so you might want to find out a little more from them before dismissing their input. Why not give it a try?

The Bible tells us to **only be united with believers**. If you think you're going to date unbelievers and marry a believer, you're deceiving yourself. The woman's mantra of "I can change him after we get married" is a foolish delusion! Throw it out the window with the commode! Change is inevitable, yes. But you want a firm foundation and good starting point to begin the adventure of a shared life in the first place, not a pre-planned intent of putting someone else on a potter's wheel to refit him into what you want him to be from the start! God's Word asks a provocative question which demands an answer: "Can two walk together unless they are agreed?" (Amos 3:3).

The journey of marriage is joyful and rewarding, but it is also challenging and difficult. The process of two different people trying to walk in step with one another is like being in a three legged race. Remember Field Day at school? Two people get together, each tying one of their legs to the other person's leg, then, putting their arm around each other, they try to get a rhythm going, trying to synchronize their movements so they can run together. The goal is to cross the finish line before the others who are also trying to run with their legs tied together. It is difficult at first. The key to a successful race is finding someone who is roughly the same height and has the same leg length as you so you can be better matched to one another for what lies ahead - and one of you must lead. Not take over, but be the one to signal the direction and timing of the move. Once that particular race is over however, the one who was the leader in that race may not be the best choice to lead the next event. The best leader in the three-legged race may not be the best leader for the egg toss! ☺ Skill in one area does not necessarily carry over to other arenas.

It is the same in marriage. Yes, we all have differences – between personalities and between men's and women's perspectives. But there are key things that we should agree upon if we are going to walk or run together. It is hard enough to travel that road with someone you *do* share faith and similar expectations with. Trying to navigate that path with someone who is not working with the same life principles and beliefs as you, adds stress and makes for some currents we were never meant to row against.

Understand that you and your spouse have unique strengths in different areas on purpose. There will be times when you are better suited to handle the lead. But there will be times when it is better for you to follow your spouse's lead – all in mutual co-operation for the goal you both want to reach.

The Bible warns us of a hard road when you become "unequally yoked" (1 Cor. 6:14) for some very good reasons – listen to the warning and take it to heart! The Bible is a wonderful book. I love the acronym "**B**asic **I**nstructions **B**efore **L**eaving **E**arth! The Bible is an excellent owners' manual for life! If you and your future spouse are working from different owner's manuals to begin with, it adds even more struggle and heartache to the process. You don't need that.

If you have already made those choices, and are living with the reality of these difficulties, don't give up. Discouragement does nothing positive in any situation. Trust and hope are dual allies given to us for the battles we face, we are not alone. God is a God of redemption and Grace and He will enable you to scale even the heights of self-made difficulties. Concentrate on the good stuff you share; make the effort to calmly discuss the things that you see differently. Both of you can win over any situation and hearts can be changed for the better, if you work like a team.

Use good language. If you're *"talkin'* trash", don't be surprised if other people think you *are* trash and treat you accordingly. Our mouth is designed to have enormous power with the words we say. We were designed in the image of the God Who created the universe and everything in it – just by speaking a few words! Our words can have a tremendous impact on our world. Are we using that power to tear other people down? Are we using our mouths to fill the sewer with more junk and getting ourselves splattered with it in the process? Be kind and gentle in your talk. People will have no way of seeing you as trashy and promiscuous if your words don't lead them to that conclusion.

One of the most powerful testimonies I ever heard about a person's words came from the first funeral I attended after I joined our church: When Darryl died, everyone was invited to share personal stories of how he had most impacted their lives. One of the guys came forward and told everyone that he previously had a problem with telling dirty jokes. He reasoned that if it was "just the guys" around to hear it, it wasn't doing any harm. During one of these times, Darryl had interrupted them and said, "Wait a minute. If the joke you're about to tell is something I can't turn around and tell my little Angela, then I don't want to hear it", and he meant it. He refused to participate in dirty language, off-color or sexual innuendo type "humor".

That testimony affected everyone in that group of men and

everyone sitting in the funeral that day that heard this man's testimony and my life forever. It raised the bar, so to speak. It was a perfect example of godly, gentle reproof and changed my perspective on one aspect of the power of my words. My words show others what kind of person I am – no matter what group of people I am with. I stopped telling dirty jokes myself after that, and gradually stopped laughing when others told them. That one statement changed a big part of my life.

Don't allow yourself to be talked into sex before marriage. It is crucial for you to understand that if the guy is pressuring you to get physical with him before the wedding, that he's not your friend – and he's not looking out for your protection or your reputation. I have known girls that have given into this lie. When the girl reacts to the change in relationship from platonic to intimate by getting more clingy, wanting to spend more and more time with him, he bolts, leaving her broken and guilty. If he says he's gonna leave if he doesn't have sex with you – let him go or let him realize that you think more of yourself and your relationship to wreck it that way. You can only give that part of you once; once you make that choice, that part of you is gone forever. It is the most personal gift you can give to your spouse on your wedding day. Someone who really loves you will wait.

Modern day clichés about "why buy the cow if you can get the milk for free?" and "trying out the mattress before you buy the bed" are smokescreens that justify a lack of commitment and cheapen the relationship. I am not speaking from a position of self-righteousness on this one, but one of experience. I did it wrong. My lack of restraint and falling for that culturally correct drivel led to the most painful damage in my life. I was blessed in God's grace to have been rescued from some of the more detrimental consequences when I made choices against God's will and Wisdom.

My husband and I have been married for 27 years now. We respect one another. We deeply love one another. We've hurt one another too. It hasn't been easy, but it's been worth the effort to learn to walk in a new level of commitment with one another. It could have turned out much differently. Start your relationships on the right foot.

If that decision has already been made, and you are no longer a virgin, today is a new day and you can make better choices in the here and now. Lust, pornography and other kinds of sexual sin are deeply harmful to everyone. But there is healing here too. There are many resources in tape, book and DVD form on retaining – and regaining – sexual purity for both men and women. Kirk Franklin's "Freedom" testimony (www.porntopurity.com), Shannon Ethridge's "Every Woman's Battle" (www.shannonethridge.com/), Stephen Arterburn's "Every Man's Battle" (www.newlife.com) and many others can give you the encouragement and support to make good choices for your life where sexual purity and personal safety are concerned. It's not too late. You are far too precious to believe otherwise!

Beside the emotional toll of giving in too early and with the wrong person, are the physical consequences. Pregnancy is something that should be a celebration, not a dread. But that's far from the only consideration. STD's are rampant. Some of them cause damage that can be cured by antibiotics, but some of them are permanent - and some of them are deadly. Don't risk it.

The people who are proponents of "safe sex" are selling condoms. And birth control pills. And magazines. And lots of other things. They will not be there for you when you are in the doctor's office getting the results of your tests. They will not be there to hold you while you sit in stunned silence while your mind runs through hoops and hurdles of "what nows" as you hear about treatment options and side effects.

One night of irresponsibility and lack of self-control can have lasting consequences that effect not only you, but your future spouse, your children, or lack of ability to have one. It can impact things you are not thinking are important at the time: bath time, kiddie pools, sharing popsicles - or kisses. Personal responsibility in the form of abstinence is absolutely your best option. Jumping off a building with a parachute that is faulty and claiming safety because you're wearing one is suicide.

Trying something to see if you can get by with it without experiencing the forewarned consequences is like Russian roulette – one day, the bullet will be in the chamber. Sterility, future miscarriages, disease and death are not what's going through your mind in the heat of those kinds of moments. It should be. Respect yourself. Respect the idea of how precious you are and that you are worth more than a "quickie". God created you personally with purpose and great forethought. He gave you the talents and gifts that make you uniquely you. Treasure that.

A song by Steve Green impacted my view on this many years ago and I want to share it with you:

Guard Your Heart

Oh, be careful little eyes what you see
Oh, be careful little eyes what you see
For the Father up above
Is looking down in love
Oh, be careful little eyes what you see

What appears to be harmless glance
Can turn to romance
And homes are divided
Feelings that should never have been awakened within
Tearing the heart in two
Listen, I beg of you

Guard your Heart
Guard your Heart
Don't trade it for treasure
Don't give it away

Guard your Heart
Guard your Heart
As a payment for pleasure
It's high price to pay
For a soul that remains sincere with conscience clear
Guard your Heart

The human heart is easily swayed
And often betrayed at the hand of emotion
You dare not leave the outcome to chance
You must choose in advance
Or live with the agony
Such needless tragedy

Guard your Heart
Guard your Heart
Don't trade it for treasure
Don't give it away

Guard your Heart
Guard your Heart
As a payment for pleasure
It's high price to pay
For a soul that remains sincere with conscience clear
Guard your Heart[2]

This song is based on Proverbs 4:23 that clearly tell us why this perspective is critical: "Guard and keep your heart with all vigilance and above all that you guard, for out of it flows the springs of life." If you keep junk out of your well, you will have clear running water – clear thinking, yielding clear and life-giving choices. If you allow your well to be polluted, it will poison your life. And there is much to guard against happening all around us!

Smokescreens

Society throws up smokescreens to change the perspective you see. It doesn't change the facts, it just muddies the water. Please don't forget – they are selling something! Condoms, birth control pills, abortion, medications for STD's and depression are all multi-**billion** dollar enterprises! Of course they will minimize responsible conduct – their profit margin depends on it! They use intellectual smokescreens like calling it "reproductive freedom". What is so freeing about multiple miscarriages? Sterility? Hemorrhaging in an emergency room somewhere? That's not reproductive anything. It *uses* your reproductive organs, but it hurts the body, soul and spirit of the women and men involved. Abortion deprives another human being of the chance to live and contribute to our mutual existence, and affects others around us who have no opportunity to experience alternative choices of life. The Bible speaks truly when it says clearly in Proverbs 16:25: "There is a way that seems right to a man and appears straight before him, but at the end of it is the way of death". Please do not allow the apparent nobility of these deceptive smokescreens lead you to deadly conclusions:

"It's a woman's choice over her own body". No. The woman's (and man's) choices are all the other things that I listed earlier about how to dress, how you see yourself, how you interact with others, where you go and who you go with. Once a baby is on the way, it is no longer your body alone. You are responsible for another life that you helped create.

Medical research shows that as early as Day 22 in utero (DAY not week!) the baby's heart is pumping his own blood through the placenta for nourishment – and it is often a different blood type! That is not an "extension" of you or a lump of non-specific tissue. It is distinctly different from you. You need to cherish that distinction.

What will you say when you have to justify extermination of the miracle of life growing inside you? Don't live with the regret I and so many others have experienced by our own lack of restraint and the resultant fumbling to avoid the natural results!

Life is sacred. It is not something to be treated lightly or disregarded. Jesus warned us "with the same measure you use for others, that measure will be dealt again to you." (Matt 7:2) The context is talking about attitudes toward other people. If you devalue someone else's life, you can expect others to devalue yours. Avoid that kind of thinking like the plague!

"Abortion should be allowed in the case of rape or incest". The facts and statistics of the matter are most cases of rape do not result in pregnancy. In the rare cases when it does, does killing another human being suddenly become justified? James Robison, who was a product of rape when his mother was in her 40's, has a lot to say about the matter. He is a world-wide evangelist, has begun many feeding and well-drilling programs in several different countries, has begun and contributes to rescue organizations that save children and teens out of sex trafficking and forced prostitution, and has had a wide-reaching impact including many other incredible contributions to our world. How would the millions of people who have been impacted by his lifetime of ministry and compassionate help be affected if his mother had successfully aborted him because of what happened to her? And he is only one man – what about the others? Hundreds of other people I have

talked to and heard about are the result of "unintended" pregnancies. The circumstances leading up to their conception do not alter the sacredness of their lives. A man I knew who ran for public office in our district, is staunchly pro-life for this very reason. Check out You Tube and listen to the girls who are abortion survivors – one had a twin who was aborted, but she survived [3], another was a survivor of a late-term saline abortion procedure [4]! There are many others. One wrong action does not justify another, it compounds the problem. Life is precious – protect it. (And vote for those who do!) The challenge Gianna Jessen issued to legislators during her address in Queen's Hall in Victoria Australia in 2008 is nothing short of miraculous – and life-changing. It also leads to the dissection of another smoke screen.

"Abortion should be an option for families who find out that there is something wrong with the baby." We dare not try to stand on the foundation of this kind of arrogance, believing it is some kind of moral "high ground"! What about the times when doctors have misdiagnosed birth defects and the children are born perfectly normal? Many people are coming forward and telling their testimonies of when testing showed problems and they decided to go through with the pregnancy anyway, trusting God for the outcome. There are times when the baby is born with nothing at all out of place and the doctors are stumped as to why the test results said otherwise. At times, physical medical conditions were operable in some amazing prenatal and peri-natal surgeries that were stunning in their intricacies and effectiveness! We cannot ignore these instances! Decisions made in fear are bound to bring heartache!

What about the children who have not been "perfectly normal" but have increased and deepened the love and impact of their families? Compassion and cooperation are powerful and life-changing testimonies in the family and to all who come in contact with these success stories rising from challenges in these situations.

Some families who had previously been disconnected and distracted by an aimless existence before the challenge of a special needs child brought out of them and to them more blessing than they would have believed possible! Yes, it takes more support and encouragement, to be sure. But that doesn't mean these children should be exterminated for someone else's idea of convenience. Check out Joni and Friends (named for its founder Joni Eareckson Tada) and other special needs support organizations online or on TV sometime! With the support and godly encouragement of fellow believers and people who have been in the same shoes, it is amazing (amazing is too dull a word to describe what I have seen in their faces!) what can happen if we trust God to complete the work He begins!

There are so many options before a pregnancy occurs to keep from having to make decisions that end someone else's life! There are also many options after the pregnancy begins. Pregnancy care centers like BirthRight and CareNet help prospective parents with counseling and resources for their next few decisions. Ultrasound machines prove what some people try to hide from scared, unknowing girls – the *life* they are carrying. These pregnancy care centers provide baby clothes, formula, diapers and many other baby supplies donated for the expected needs of these new moms and dads, along with counseling, education, loving support and encouragement - all free of charge - so new parents are not left feeling alone in the struggles of new parenthood.

They also share accurate information on adoption. Things are very different in the adoption process than most of us may think.

In Marilyn Meberg's book, "I'd Rather Be Laughing", she tells the story of how her daughter Beth, whom they adopted when she was very young, had a reunion with her birth parents and got to meet her biological family. They share in one another's lives even now, spending time with one another. It is a very moving example of alternate possibilities I had not been open to earlier in my life because of base-less fears. Information is power. It dismantles fear.

Even with all this information, some still say that "Being 'pro-choice' is better than taking away other people's options on what they are allowed to do." I find it ironic that some people who call themselves "pro-choice" adamantly ridicule people who believe in the preciousness of life. Life is a choice. Why are they opposed to *that* choice?

They label others "anti-abortion", like that is something bad. Those who favor killing pre-born infants call those with opposing views "anti-", while they sound "pro". You can tell in a New York minute when listening to the news which side of things the reporters are on by how they term the respective sides of the debate. They call themselves "pro-choice", not pro-abortion or pro-death, while they sneer at pro-life proponents, calling them "anti-abortion activists". It's no less than Orwellian "new speak". Changing what you call it doesn't change what it is. It is murder plain and simple - a murder for the sake of convenience.

The first step to healing is acknowledging what really happens in these procedures—a beating heart within a living, moving, growing body is pulled apart in what is supposed to be the safest place on earth, the womb. The heart of the intended mother is broken with regret and remorse when she comes to grips with what really happened. And the world loses what would have been the contribution and inspiration of another precious life on our planet. Acknowledging these facts, and taking responsibility for each of our own actions, can prevent this tragedy.

If this choice has already been made in your life, and the remorse feels too great to bear, you don't have to stay there, stuck with the guilt and regret! The freedom of being set free from condemnation and self-recrimination is a blessed peace and joy that cannot be adequately explained, but is a gift beyond measure for anyone who reaches out and grabs hold of it! It is yours for the asking!

All Life is Sacred

I would also like to interject here that murder is murder no matter who the victim is. The media, using the murders of pro-abortion doctors and the bombings of abortion clinics, raise battle cries that "prove" that pro-life defenders are unstable and a danger to society. Pro-life people are not murderers. The murder of George Tiller and others, and the bombings of abortion clinics are flat out wrong. The wheels of justice were turning in the courtroom to bring to light the horrendous reality of what happens in these legally sanctioned tombs of death. Even with Roe v Wade and the resultant laws allowing abortion, there are still laws and requirements for the hows and wherefores that are not being followed in these places. The legal system was working toward George Tiller's imprisonment and the closing of his clinic on the basis of his breaking the law in these areas. His murder and other instances where people have taken similar extreme measures to enforce anti-abortion beliefs adds to the wrong done and gives pro-death activists excuses for denigrating and discounting pro-life principles.

Pro-life means life is sacred. If George Tiller had been convicted on multiple counts of murder and had been executed for genocide by operating an illegal abortion clinic, it would have happened as the legal and established consequences of civil and criminal government that is set up for that specific purpose, not a free-lance vigilante taking the law into his own hands. Tiller's murder was no less wrong than that of pro-life proponent Jim Pouillon, who was murdered, gunned down during a peaceful event, as a direct result of his pro-life stand. Even though the "contributions" to society of both men differ on opposing poles of the spectrum, both deserve equal protection under that law.

I haven't experienced the overwhelming emotion that arises if someone you love had been injured or killed by someone else in this manner, but I can sympathize that it could push you to do horrible things that you normally would not think yourself capable of. But that's where Grace and Faith comes in.

Grace gives you the ability to run to God for the pain that is twisting you into something you don't want to be, and Faith assures you that God is fully capable of handling the situation. Pray your knees off! And Trust that God's plan for you is not to take someone else's life. If you want to defend life legally, there are many wonderful organizations that can help you do just that – and many people who will dig deep into their pockets and fund these organizations to get legal justice against these heinous crimes.

We have freedom of speech in this country – not freedom to play God. That job is too big for any of us to fill anyway. But God can and will use us to help, encourage and support one another in tough times!

The Next Generation

When my daughter, Jennifer began her first year in high school, her freshman Civics teacher told them they would be writing a term paper as the major assignment for the class. They were able to choose any topic they wanted, but they needed to truly research the subject and show the sources they garnered their information from and declare the conclusions they arrived at as a result. He left the subject material open to the students' choice, and cautioned that choosing a controversial topic needed to be backed up with facts, not just a rant of "this is what I think", or "everybody knows..."

My daughter chose the topic of abortion. (She never took the easy way out of anything!) Jenn knew about some basic information, but I hadn't gotten into details with her at this point about my own personal story on the subject, as she was only 14 years old. When I started to direct her to resources, assuming she had already decided which side of the debate she was on for herself, she stopped me short. "Mom, stop. I know how you feel about it. I know what my teachers say about it. I know what other people and my friends say about it. I'm not going to listen to any of you. I don't care what any of you think. I am going to do this on my own and if, after I've done all this research I don't think abortion is wrong, then so be it. I am going to do this on my own."

I got a lump in my throat and fear got right in my face. How could she say she didn't care what I thought? How could she...? She didn't have any idea what it felt like to miscarry three times and almost lose the two children I did have. Of course not! She hadn't experienced anything like that - Thank

God! But it was obvious there would be no discussion at this point. I needed to let her do this her way. Somehow, I stifled the flood of tears and words I wanted to pour out at that moment, and prayed! It wasn't my assignment, it was hers; I needed to let her do it.

She went online. She went to the school library. She listened to experts. She wrote for what felt like an eternity - she wouldn't let me see any of it until it was all done and graded. I was worried about how she would process the information she picked up without my input - yes, I know. How very self-centric of me. I am Mom, and protection is both instinctive and an important maternal attribute for which I will never apologize. It was the late 90's and I was concerned about the influence of the "I, me, mine, now!" mentality that measures morals situationally against how someone feels at the moment instead of as an anchor to keep someone from drifting into dangerous waters of peer pressure, "tolerance" and convenience. I had been in those waters; I didn't want my kids anywhere near them! I should have had more confidence in the truth of the matter. Honestly researched, sifting through the medical and physical facts of the matter, she came to her own conclusion.

I remember her coming home from school that day and handing me her paper. I remember a red A- on the face of the plain typed title page and reading what she wrote. I cried. After 14 pages, complete with footnotes and bibliography, her conclusion was as direct as humanly possible, and it is burned into my memory: "It doesn't matter what anyone else says. Abortion is murder, plain and simple."

Anyone who looks at the medical facts and physiological progression from conception to birth has no choice but to come to the same conclusion. Science has long ago proven what we could not see happening in every pregnant woman's womb – even at the time of Roe v. Wade. Ultra sounds and fiber-optic cameras clearly show what the pro-abortion defense wants to hide so desperately: Life.

If you need to see the truth of it in front of your own eyes, check out the exhibit at the Oregon Museum of Science and Industry in Portland Oregon. We went there in 2010 with my daughter's family for the day. One of the displays shows the complete cycle of embryonic growth of a human being at each stage of development in a tour around the room.

As I was explaining to my three-year old grandson that these were "dolls that showed what babies look like when they are growing in their mommy's bellies", I saw a sign that countered my explanation and in fact verified they were actually preserved human fetuses. As I looked more carefully at each one, I could tell which ones were male and which ones were female after a certain stage of development and found myself praying for them.

I was horrified at first when I realized they are not models, and still have mixed feelings about each of their remains being displayed like that. But there is no denying who they were, regardless of their size. They had fingers and toes, and everything else they needed. Some with hair, some were bald; so tiny and fragile, but absolutely growing individual people. They had been souls meant to be cherished and now were dry, empty shells, declaring their existence now more loudly than they could have earlier in their lives, and I grieved for what was lost. Life is precious – no matter how tiny.

Reality Check

To the senators and representatives that throw this debate around like a political football, justifying their own stance by stating they are "not forcing their personal views on others" as their reason for not defending the unborn on the floors of their respective houses, I offer this thought. By allowing abortion in the face of so many other alternatives, and in the light of the medical technology that proves undoubtedly that life does indeed begin at conception, are you not turning a blind eye to the fact that men and women who "choose" abortion are in fact *permanently* "forcing their own personal views" on their pre-born children? How is that any different than other things you've seen fit to legislate, like child abuse, or neglect, or even the recent laws you've made about controlling what we are allowed to eat, or smoke, or use because it bothers or hurts someone else?

You've legislated the elimination of snack food and soda from school vending machines, and have begun government initiated removal of parental custody over child obesity, calling it a form of abuse. You've banned smoking in public places, increased "sin taxes" on cigarettes and alcohol, supposedly to pay for the increased medical services the government pays for in smoke- and alcohol-related disease treatment. You mandate the stupidest requirements for labeling things to preempt ludicrous law suits that should be thrown out as laughable: "Caution: this lawnmower should not be picked up and used as a hedge trimmer or you could lose your fingers" and "Sleeping pills may cause drowsiness". DUH!

But you've remained stunningly silent in the face of the carnage that is happening all over our country, ruining lives and calling it a right. How is that logical?

If a woman, on her way to an abortion clinic, stops at a convenience store and is shot in a robbery attempt and her baby dies, the would-be robber is charged with felony murder of the child. As he should be! But if that same woman makes it the next two blocks to the clinic and has it done in a "medical" facility, the baby's death is legal? How does that make sense? The child is still dead, but there is no outcry – no one voting for their protection, in their defense – on the premise that you don't feel comfortable legislating against personal freedom? Some people are too weak to save themselves, they need heroes. They need defenders who will fight for them. You are in that office for such a time as this.

Proverbs 24: 11-12 is your wake up call, as it is mine: "Deliver those who are drawn away to death, and those who totter to the slaughter, hold them back [from their doom]. If you [profess ignorance and] say, Behold, we did not know this, does not He Who weighs and ponders the heart perceive and consider it? And He Who guards your life, does not He know it? And shall not He render to [you and] every man according to his works?"

Talk to abortion survivors; watch the interviews on You Tube. Abortion hurts deeply. Worse than second-hand smoke, worse than obesity, worse than soda pop or sugary snacks in the lunchroom, abortion kills one person and permanently affects the other for the rest of their lives. You are in positions of great influence for a reason. You will one day be accountable to God for your votes. Do you honestly want to stand before Him knowing what you know and not have fought for life?

As long as there is life there is hope, and if we are still breathing we can change our ways – Scrooge dropped his Marley-esque chains and lived a completely different life! So can we! I don't want to hear the word "unforgiven" facing a grim reaper at the grave! I want to stand before God in the hereafter, knowing I took the opportunity He offered, to make different choices and live a better life! Don't you?

To the proponents of abortion who cry out for the right to end the lives of their children, calling it "reproductive freedom", I plead with you - hear the same verse and add to it one more: "For you, brethren, were [indeed] called to freedom; only [do not let your] freedom be an incentive to your flesh and an opportunity or excuse [for selfishness], but through love you should serve one another." (Galatians 5:13) You are free not to have sex, you are free to use "effective" birth control, you are free to give any infant resulting from your lack of self-control up for adoption to any number of willing couples who dearly want to share their love and wealth and knowledge with young lives who want to be given the same opportunity you were for life and breath and freedom to make *their* own choices.

I made wrong choices earlier in my life. Some of them I have been able to change. I deeply regret the ones I can do nothing about. Understand and see the end of the road you're on. Listen to women like Gianna Jessen, Claire Culwell, Abby Johnson, and Jill Stanek. Hear their hearts. Abortion is not a "right". It's not pretty, it's not reproductive, and it's not freedom. But there is a way to true freedom – without regret. It stands in the path of Life, and there are millions of people willing to help you find it, if you will only listen. <3

Forgiveness and Healing

God has put many special people and situations in my life that have gotten me from the crippling remorse and guilt to the freedom and peace of mind concerning this issue and the circumstances that I am living with today. In going back to my high school, visiting with the sisters who were there back then and meeting new ones, I am gifted by my relationship with them. In connection with them, I have met other women who are associated with BirthRight. Together, they are teaching and sharing God's love with a new generation of girls about the Truth of the preciousness of Life.

Through extensive TV programming on PBS, Discovery Channel and other science venues, I have seen the undeniable progression of life. In connection with the church I attend right now, I met others who work with the CareNet Pregnancy Centers. EWTN and TBN and Daystar and the internet have introduced me to Silent No More, Priests for Life, National Pro-Life Alliance, Operation Rescue, Americans United For Life, Rachel's Vineyard, Concerned Women for America, and many other groups who defend life, educate about abortion, and help women and their families heal after abortion has taken place. No two people are the same, no two situations fit exactly for each person. But the commonalities can bring us together to defend life - Life of the unborn and lives left scarred by their deaths. There is help.

I have found personally that everyone deals with issues differently. Just as we all have differences in personalities and communication; we all have different ways of dealing with death. Some work well for some people but only add to the pain for others. In my journey of healing, some very well-meaning and precious people have said that part of the healing process of post-abortive women requires us to name our children. They say that you *need* to do that to heal properly. I took their advice and began the task of naming each of my four children that I never got to hold in my arms, beginning with my first, whom I aborted. It hurt to go back there after having made peace with God and the situation some time ago. But I pressed through with it, believing at the time that it was something essential to my healing.

I chose a name that could be used for a boy or a girl, as I didn't know which group I should be choosing from. I went on a few days later to name my second child with the same criteria. It was even harder. It became more painful instead of bringing the expected peace of mind. I didn't know what to do.

When I went to my husband, and told him what I had been doing, he asked me to stop. He felt it would do nothing but increase the pain from this point on. I prayed and sensed his wisdom in my situation. Not that we should think that an increased sensitivity is necessarily an indication we are doing something we shouldn't; sometimes it hurts more before it is made whole. But in this case, there were other factors to consider.

My first two children were brought to life in the time before my husband's relationship with me. It was important for me to name them to complete the acceptance of their loss from my life and be able to acknowledge them from my heart. But I felt the truth of what my husband was saying about the children we lost in our miscarriages. Maybe the timing has just not arrived for us to do that yet.

God knows all my children. He cradles them in His arms. Someday I will meet them all and find out what God named them. I didn't need to go through that extra step to know that God forgave me the first time I asked Him to and is giving me His peace. For others, I am told that naming their children was crucial in their restoration. That is fine too. I truly believe there is more than one way to be healed and restored.

When Jesus healed several blind people in the gospels, He used different methods for each one: for one He simply declared it, for another He touched them, for another He made mud with spit, for another He told them to wash. For some, the healing was instantaneous, for others it came in stages, like the man who said that first he saw men as trees, and then after another touch from Jesus, he saw clearly. (Mark 8:23-25)

Each person was different. Each one was healed differently. They were all healed. We can be completely healed too. Some pain is so deep it takes different levels to heal around each one. It's not that God isn't strong enough to do it all at once; He emphatically is. But He knows that we are more fragile in certain areas and He takes a tender and metered Hand to make sure we are not overcome in the process.

So it was with me.

Healing in Layers

God took a lot of baby steps with me. He took years to show me that I was precious to Him, that He made me on purpose, that I was not an accident, that He is always with me and will never leave me nor forsake me, that my worth to Him is not based on what I've done, but on the fact that He is My Father, and He loves me. I've known these verses for years now. They have anchored my soul and given me a rock to stand on.

I can do things now that I could not do before: I can celebrate with women enjoying a new baby again. I can work in the nursery. I can talk about my experience without breaking down in sobs – a few tears here and there, but I figure that's healthy at this point.

I made so many advances in attitudes and emotions since this journey began that I thought I was done. I thought, after all this time, the healing was completed. Now that I could write this to share with others and my testimony was near completion, I thought I was "over it all".☺ I was wrong. God was preparing me for the final release from the last of those chains –

In recent months, I had attended a Care Net fundraising banquet at UCONN and had the opportunity to meet the local director of two Care Net facilities in my area. The festivities of the evening were coming to a close and I wanted to let her know how much I appreciated what she said. There were pictures to be taken and thank yous to be said, so my comments were brief, but when our eyes locked after a hug we both knew we needed to meet again in a more private setting.

Two weeks later I called her and set up a meeting after I got out of work. We talked for a while and she showed me a book. It was a 12-week post-abortion healing study written by a woman named Linda Cochrane called "Forgiven and Set Free". "That's nice," I thought. "I don't need that anymore, I'm good. But I am glad you have a good resource to share with other people now."

Pati told me about her own journey through the study and I thought afterward how powerful her testimony about it was, but I had no intention of doing it myself. The reason I had come was to make my own story available for others. But I did want to keep talking with her. Being able to openly talk about our individual experiences and how it affected us was not "polite dinner conversation", but it brought a release I couldn't get in any other way. I hadn't been able to be transparent about this in a while. We decided to meet again the following week.

At our next meeting, she asked me if I had prayed about doing the study and I laughed: "No. it never occurred to me to pray about it." She commented that at least that was an honest answer.☺ But something had changed: over the previous week; it became evident it was not something I was going to be able to sidestep. God put this thing on my heart, not trying to "talk me into it", but simply declaring I would be truly free at the end of it. The decision process happened without any input from me; God changed my heart on the matter. There was no doubt I would do the study.

Two weeks after that, I had been editing the "final draft" of The Power of Choices, and was started into chapter two of the study. Piece of cake so far. Nothing new here, God has taken me through all this before.

When I got to the section on "God, Our Righteousness", I found some of the same scriptures I read a bunch of times about Jesus being the Righteous Branch and how He "did not come into this world to save the righteous". What happened next could be nothing less than the two-edged sword of the Spirit – as in Hebrews 4:12: "For the word of God is alive and active. Sharper than any double-edged sword, it penetrates even to dividing soul and spirit, joints and marrow; it judges the thoughts and attitudes of the heart."

It was such a strange feeling. It kind of felt like being part of dissecting my own thoughts - like they belonged to someone else. There was no pain in it; just a sudden release from a blind spot that I realized did not need to be there anymore. Before I knew what was happening, God faced me with the lies I had been *telling myself* for years, getting comfortable with and accepting as fact. This locked-off area in my mind made the memories of my abortion experience feel more noble—more tolerable to look back on with less accountability.

I was faced with the bare truth of *my* choices, unvarnished and putrid. I was seeing it through different eyes. I had seen myself before as a victim of someone else's ultimatum, now that (last?) deception could be exposed.

The word Sorrow came to mind, and I typed it in to Bible Gateway to find part of a verse. God gave me what I could not have anticipated – and more. I read verse after verse that spoke of His Grace for my sin: Ps 31:10, Ps 32:10, Ps 34:18, and then came Ps 51:17: "My sacrifice [the sacrifice acceptable] to God is a broken spirit; a broken and a contrite heart [broken down with **sorrow** for sin and humbly and thoroughly penitent], such, O God, You will not despise."

It was safe to confess the last, darkest secret.

"I acknowledged my sin to You, and my iniquity I did not hide. I said, I will confess my transgressions to the Lord [*continually unfolding* the past till all is told]--then You [*instantly*] forgave me the guilt and iniquity of my sin. Selah [pause, and calmly think of that]!" (Psalm 32:5, emphasis mine)

It was quicker than immediately – it was pre-emptive: it was back-pedaling to rush forward! God already knew, I wasn't telling Him anything He hadn't already seen. He had been there with me the whole time – even in that examination room - and He still loved me deeply and completely. He was giving me the chance to show Him my wound so He could "instantly" take it away. After 32 years.

I knew more than I let on about my baby's development before I aborted. I had told everyone (and finally began to believe it myself) that I really didn't know. I've said it for years. But right in the front of my mind somehow, with the assurance that "Jesus did not come to save the righteous" (which means He came to save the unrighteous! And I knew absolutely that is me!), I needed to be honest about the *whole* situation, or I knew I would still be trapped by these grave clothes stinking like a mummy and crawling with...(I don't know what!)

I purposely did NOT try to find out exactly how much of my baby was already formed at that point. I didn't *want* to know specifics because that wouldn't have fit in with my plans of "freedom" and "carefree-ness" away from responsibilities. I refused to find out specifics at the time, so I wouldn't be talked out of it. I knew my baby was more than just a lump of cells. I knew most of what I had later seen on TV. I was hammered with the truth of it when I saw that "Miracle of Life" episode on NOVA. The act was already done, I couldn't undo it. That was why I had reacted so badly at the time. But enough time had gone by, by the time I saw the video, that I could "back claim" some kind of ignorance and continue lying to myself about my own part in it. The truth of the matter was, I let my "boyfriend" push me in the direction that I wanted to go, and his ultimatum gave me the outlet for not accepting the blame for what I wanted to do but felt too guilty about doing on my own. Denial was a hiding place to protect my sanity until God had completed the rest of His healing to keep me from being overwhelmed by that ugly truth.

That thought sickened me that day, but God's Grace was right there reminding me "weeping may endure for a night, but Joy comes in the morning" (Ps 30:50) . I realized then, in admitting it, it lost its power on my heart! I cried. And I felt His instant comfort - just like He promised.

As I continue through the rest of this study I know that I won't have a nervous breakdown or be overwhelmed, but, taking one step at a time, I surely will be set free from the weight of all the rest of it in God's mercy and Grace.

I can try turning my back on the unpleasantness of it all, attempting to move on without taking care of this once and for all. That has always been an option. But nothing compares to this saving Truth. Jesus *became* sin, so that I could *be* His

Righteousness. (2 Cor. 5:21) He bore my shame on the cross *because He wanted to set me free*. No matter what I say out loud, the Spirit of God living in me knows the truth.

It was something that I didn't want to face. It had festered all this time, under the surface. The truth won't stay hidden in the light - but it can be redeemed. I am not the same person I was back then, God has been faithful in His perseverance not to let me go, and He keeps saying, "the old has passed away and all things are made new", "His mercies are new every morning".

As soon as I became willing to take ownership of that truth, He lifted it off me so I wouldn't be crushed under the weight of it. I felt it. "For godly grief and the pain God is permitted to direct, produce a repentance that leads and contributes to salvation and deliverance from evil, and it never brings regret; but worldly grief (the hopeless **sorrow** that is characteristic of the pagan world) is deadly [breeding and ending in death]." (2 Cor. 7:10 AMP) That is the gift I was given again this morning.

In Jesus, the sin we have done is condemned while the spirit inside us is made alive and runs forward to Him! Don't exchange sure fulfillment of the choices made for Life and the blessings and protection of God for the false promises of acceptance, validation and "love" whispered in the dark – it's a lie that will cause more pain than you ever want to know!

I beg of you to learn from others, so that you do not have to personally experience the kind of regret I had to be healed from! Yes, the reason I am the person I am today is greatly influenced by what I have experienced along my journey. But believe me when I tell you it is much better to side-step some pathways than to walk through them.

But if you do – or did, like me – don't stay stuck in that lie. You can begin again, right where you are! You can know Joy and Peace and real Love. God already provided the way out of that pit – forgiveness through Jesus Christ. New life comes from death – His for yours.

In retrospect, there are things I have experienced in the middle of this journey I could have gotten no other way – and these I am grateful for. I am grateful for the people I have met and who have helped me in the healing process. I am grateful to know my husband knows my darkest moments and loves me dearly still. I am grateful that I can use my testimony to comfort someone else who can't yet express how deeply this hurts, and to be able to assure her that God's Grace is the only thing that can heal pain that profound. I don't just think so, I *know* it; I've experienced it for myself. I am grateful to be able to share that.

I have perspective now at 48 to see things much more clearly than I did at 17 and 18 (of course). I recently heard Erwin McManus, lead pastor at Mosaic, in Los Angeles speaking on Joyce Meyer's program "Enjoying Everyday Life". He said something profound about Freedom: "We think we want the freedom to choose... The real power in life is not the freedom to choose, but making choices that give you Freedom"! I can testify to the simply pivotal Truth of this in my own life and heartily shout "Amen"!

Many people, like me can also testify that choosing poorly brings regret. The apostle Paul had many regrets. It was not empty writing when he wrote to the Romans, "...since they did not see fit to acknowledge God or approve of Him or consider him worth knowing, God gave them over to a base and condemned mind to do things not proper or decent but loathsome..." (Romans 1:27, 28).

All of us have been there at one time or another to differing degrees: "Since all have sinned and are falling short of the honor and glory which God bestows and receives" (Romans 3:23). The temptation to give into the condemnation is stronger some days than others. We have lots of reasons for the guilt and shame we feel. But thank God we don't have to stay there! He is a heart-beat, a whispered prayer of repentance away!

"Therefore [there is] now no condemnation (no adjudging guilty of wrong) for those who are in Christ Jesus, who live [and] walk not after the dictates of the flesh, but after the dictates of the Spirit, for the law of the Spirit of life [which is] in Christ Jesus [the law of the new being] has freed me from the law of sin and of death. For God has done what the Law could not do, [its power] being weakened by the flesh [the entire nature of man without the Holy Spirit], Sending His own Son in the guise of sinful flesh and as an offering for sin, [God] condemned sin in the flesh [subdued, overcame, deprived it of its power over all who would accept that sacrifice]" (Romans 8:1-3).

This is my experience and heart on the matter: Listen to well-meaning protectors of Life, hold dear their friendship and share their love of Jesus. Be encouraged by their tenderness and passion for life. Understand the process may take a different course for you than it did for others. And when you are feeling the release from your weight, and want to share that gift with other hurting women, know that others may need more time or different pathways than you did.

For the guidance you need for your own personal healing, go to The Source. God will lead you in all Truth. He will let you know what to follow for yourself and what is a path that may be different for someone else. He knows. He heals. I am proof. I am not alone. Make the choices God gifts you with.

Looking back at my mid-teens in retrospect, the speed of my progression from innocently dating a boy in my youth group at 15, to the downward spiral my subsequent choices took me on was stunning! One summer, I was refusing to French kiss a blonde kid with freckles and attending a youth retreat through my church, and by the next summer, I was no longer a virgin, and my mom was threatening a 23-year-old with statutory rape charges if I wasn't back in my bedroom by nightfall. Earlier, I had dreams of a sweet sixteen party with family and friends around for the celebration. I was grounded for my 16thbirthday, for ditching my brother at the swimming hole and going to Ocean Beach with a bunch of older kids in some guy's van and coming home drunk for the first time. Not how I thought things would go - go figure.

Please understand I am **not** bragging here. I am simply issuing a warning that enough wrong choices in quick succession can dramatically alter your life, and leave you wondering how it all happened so fast. You have the power to choose – I beg of you to choose wisely!

In closing this, my testimony, let me offer you a perspective you may not have considered in quite this way before, a point of view that I told the girls that day in front of those sisters: *God is pro-choice*! God gives us free-will and has endowed us with the ability to make choices. He clearly tells us so. After two chapters of explaining the blessings of doing things His way and the curses we will bring upon ourselves if we do things against His instructions in Deuteronomy chapters 28 and 29, He puts it plainly in one sentence. In chapter 30, verse 19, He says: "I call heaven and earth to witness this day against you that I have set before you life and death, the blessings and the curses; therefore choose life that you and your descendants may live." God is pro-life. God is also pro-choice! But there is a right choice and there is a wrong choice. And, as long as you are still alive and Jesus has not come back yet, it is not too late to make the right choice! The door is still open and it's an open book test: choose life.

God Bless you.

Epilogue

I was almost done the post-abortion Bible study, "Forgiven and Set Free", wrapping up the editing on "The Power of Choices", and looking forward to the beginning of the new adventure - living life healed, after 32 years of regret. I still had a chapter and a half to go and was hanging on every word in the reading when the breakthrough of a lifetime hit me.

Fears, frustrations, resentments, and doubts all had a part of discounting and de-valuing the Grace and Peace God repeatedly told me were already mine. Instead enjoying God's gift of freedom, I used to focus on the painful memories, my wrong ways of handling certain situations, and regrets over my past. My emotions repeatedly dragged me down memory lane, throwing me into debilitating regret to the point of almost physical pain on a moment's notice. I lived like that for so long, I thought that cycle was beyond my control. Because of different teachings I had heard, I now understood that when I did this, *I was choosing* my wounded emotions over God's sovereignty and loving instruction. I was compounding my own problems, by making the first offenses more of an issue to deal with. God had paved the way for a completely different option that no on else was able to provide for me. I could *choose differently* beginning today! This one choice, open to me – and to you – at any time, is the treasure of our lifetime, and the key that unlocks all our chains and prison doors – forever. But the power to make this choice on my own seemed beyond my ability.

The key lies in the meanings of two words that made all the difference to my understanding of God's Grace and why I had thought all this time that I had already forgiven myself for choosing abortion, but was in fact still chained to the guilt and pain of that particular sin.

This key is hidden in the English language by a double-meaning phrase: "making up for". When I was a little kid, and did something wrong, I knew I needed to "make up for it". If I hit my brother, I needed to say I was sorry. If I stole something, I needed to give it back. If I damaged something, I needed to fix it, or replace it with something that wasn't broken. That was how we were told we needed to "make up for" what we did wrong. Then, the other person was supposed to say "I forgive you" or "I accept your apology". This is a simple exchange. But it groups together two different concepts into one that I needed to understand separately to be able to revel in the freedom God so dearly wants to share with us!

These two concepts are **atonement** and **restitution**. Most of the time, they happen in the same time frame, but they are very different. Both concepts can be phrased as "making up for" your wrong-doing, but *they are not interchangeable*. Not understanding this fact is the prison I was trapped in until September 2011.

I had already heard teaching that explained that the things written in the Old Testament were not just historical facts of what was required back then for the Israelites, but were all symbolic of promises that Jesus fulfilled for believers by the way He lived and died here 2000 years ago. It also incorporates instructions for us for godly living today. In fact, the apostle Paul says exactly that in 1 Cor. 10:11: "Now these things befell them by way of a figure [as an example and warning to us]; they were written to admonish and fit us for right action by good instruction..."

The books of the Old Testament go into great detail about sacrifices for a variety of different sins. Depending on the severity of the sin, different procedures were put in place to atone for it. The symbolism for most of this was pretty clear to me. We know we are not going around killing animals to "make up for" our sins. Jesus said "I desire mercy not sacrifice, Go and learn what this means" (Matt 9:13). In earlier teachings, the Bible says God "does not delight in sacrifices and sacrificial offerings" from us, in fact, He tells us the only sacrifices He will accept from us is "a broken and contrite spirit over our sins" (Psalm 51:17) and "the sacrifice of praise from our lips" (Hebrews 13:15)!

So for us, only One sacrifice fits the description of "a male ram without blemish and of the proper value" in relation to the required sacrifices for today. Jesus came to earth to **be** our guilt offering. Only Jesus Christ's atoning death on the cross can possibly cover the depravity, perverseness and degradation of my abortion – and for all the sins I committed in my life. Nothing else will do the job. He **is** the Lamb! Jesus is also the High Priest who presents the sacrifice to the Lord, and God is the One Who releases the offender - "accepts our apology." ☺ In Leviticus 6:7, He says: "And the priest shall make atonement for him before the Lord, and he shall be forgiven for anything of all he may have done by which he has become guilty." Not just *some* of my sins, not just the ones I *feel* better about after my confession, but "anything of all" by which we are "guilty"! **Forgiveness of guilt is the result of atonement**! Jesus paid it all!

That sacrifice for the "guilt offering" is complete in and of itself. It does not need augmentation or additions from me to complete it. The atonement part of "making up for" my sin is already covered by Jesus, as soon as I present my "broken and contrite spirit" to God in confession and acknowledgement for what I did.
But what about the other part? There is also the *restitution*, the replacement or restoration of the item(s) taken. According to Leviticus 6:4-5 The offender needs to replace or repay the stolen or defrauded item, (or the monetary value of that item)

plus 1/5 of its value to the previous owner. In the book, "Forgiven and Set Free", Linda Cochrane points out Numbers 5:7-8 says that if the owner, or a close relative is no longer available to make this reimbursement to, "the restitution belongs to the Lord". Ok, I get the concept of repaying what was stolen. I get it that God was the one I needed to make restitution to. But I am not dealing with a packet of gum or hotel towels or something I lifted from a store shelf. How could I make restitution for a human life? Contrary to the old saying, ignorance was *not* bliss. It was keeping me miserable. What is the symbolic parallel for this?

James says if anyone is "deficient in Wisdom", we should "ask the giving God, [Who gives] to everyone liberally and ungrudgingly, without reproaching or fault-finding, and it will be given to him" – so I asked Him, what was I missing here? I remembered a verse in the Old Testament when Samuel told Saul, "Obedience is better than sacrifice and to heed is better than the fat of rams" but he didn't stop there; he continued: "for rebellion is like the sin of divination and arrogance like the evil of idolatry." (1 Sam 15:22-23 NIV). The words "arrogance" and "idolatry" seemed to leap off the page at me, and God made the connections clear to me!

The puzzle pieces flew together and I wanted to cheer out loud!

Choosing to dwell on my painful memories over God's forgiveness was actually idolatry. My own emotions had become idols I unwillingly served that drove my joy into the dirt every time. This was not a sign of victimhood or powerlessness; it was arrogance. In my arrogance, I thought my being chained to the pain of regret somehow helped me to atone not only for the abortion, but for other things I was also beating myself up over: my disrespectful and resentful relationship with my mom, my unforgiving and dishonoring relationship with my dad, and my own self-condemnation over not being a perfect wife and mom to my husband and my children - and I didn't have a clue that is what it all was!

God tells us, "we can do all things through Him Who strengthens us." I can avail myself of the power of the Holy Sprit to tear that idol out by the roots and turn back to God in confession and release. That guilt was already atoned for and forgiven! The sacrifice of praise, dancing in the glow of His Grace, and delighting in the freedom from all of it is the only sacrifice He will accept from me.

When I insist on somehow adding my own guilt as part of the atonement, I block the process of Grace and continue to be hindered, burdened, and kept from the freedom of God's release from my chains! THAT'S what Paul is talking about when he said, "Do not allow yourselves to be enslaved again in the yoke of slavery to sin!" God's requirement for *atonement* (amends, punishment, payment) of all my sins is **fully met** in the Lamb of God. Then, that person is justified - "just as if I'd" never sinned - cleansing our consciences completely. God doesn't "keep us groveling" - **we** keep going back there! We can choose **at any time** to turn away from the sin, confess it, and then **let go of it** - *if we choose to*! I choose every day to be free of that prison or to walk into that cell again. Today I choose to live Free!

When I first began participating in 40 Days for Life, and donating to pro-life organizations and even writing this book, part of me was operating from a premise of these actions "making up for" my abortion. Because I didn't know how to make *restitution* for my abortion, I was still trying to *atone* for it! The difference in what I was trying to do all these years was finally clear when I understood "making up for" had two components!

I know I can't bring my children back. I don't need to. My aborted and miscarried children are already in heaven with

My Savior, Who paid the atonement. Restitution is *not* my trying to replace or restore them to Him; that part is done already. So restitution in this case is repayment of time. Revelation 12:11 says: "they have overcome (conquered) him by means of the blood of the Lamb and by the utterance of their testimony..." When God sets us free, it is with the stated purpose of setting us before Himself ready to serve Him in the ways He pre-ordained us to before we were born (Ephesians2:10)! The utterance of my testimony is not only restitution for me, but shining the Light of this Freedom out as a beacon for others who are in the same boat I was in! I can *gladly* make restitution, repaying time, effort, honor, respect, mercy, forgiveness, etc. to other people and to God. I can let others know my story and that once any sin – even the sin of abortion! - is confessed, God *instantly* forgives it, puts it under the atoning blood sacrifice of Christ, and removes it as far as the east is from the west, NEVER to hold it against us again!

Thank you Lord for eyes to see, ears to hear, a heart that beats for You and the Love that makes it a Joy! Thank you for others who have made these same realizations in your Grace and come back to share it with me!

Thank you for setting me Free - and for giving me the opportunity to go back to share this freedom with others! I will shout this from the rooftops: There truly is now no condemnation for those who are Christ Jesus! I am living proof!

Footnotes

[1] "Freedom From Your Past", Jimmy Evans & Ann Billington, p. 94 © 1994, 2006, 2009 by Jimmy Evans Marriage Today P.O. Box 59888 Dallas TX 75229 www.marriagetoday.com All rights reserved. Used by permission.

[2] "Guard Your Heart" by Jon Mohr © 1989 Birdwing Music (ASCAP) (adm. At EMICMCPublishing.com) All Rights reserved. Used by permission.

[3] Claire Culwell's testimony:
http://www.youtube.com/watch?v=rk0cW6MGLas

[4] Gianna Jessen's testimony:
http://www.youtube.com/watch?v=kPF1FhCMPuQ

Suggested Resources

The resources I have mentioned in this testimony are only a drop in the bucket of all the helpful materials God has used to heal my broken heart over the years! There are many others that I have not yet taken advantage of, but am currently looking into, and know people who have received great benefits from still other sources.

I heartily recommend these resources for your journey, and encourage you to explore any others that God lays on your heart and in your path.

"The Miracle of Life" PBS episode of NOVA – Emmy award winning documentary of human conception and gestation filmed by Lennart Nillsson
http://www.shoppbs.org/product/index.jsp?productI d=3450863&cp=1378003.1412584.11580310&ab=NOVABody Brain&parentPage=family

"Freedom From Your Past" by Jimmy Evans and Ann Billington, copyright 1994, 2006, 2009 by Jimmy Evans Marriage Today P.O. Box 59888 Dallas TX 75229 www.marriagetoday.com

"Overcoming Fear with Faith" by Joyce Meyer, www.joycemeyer.org

"The Life You Long For" by Beth Moore, Life Outreach International, www.lifetoday.org

"Your Scars are Beautiful to God" by Sharon Jaynes, www.sharonjaynes.com, copyright 2006 Published by Harvest House Publishers Eugene OR 97402 www.harvesthousepublishers.com recommended with permission by the author.

"Big Girls Don't Whine" by Jan Silvious copyright 2003 published by W Publishing Group, a division of Thomas Nelson, Inc P.O. Box 141000 Nashville TN 37214

"Living Free, Breaking the Cycle of Defeat" by James Robison and Robert Morris copyright 2010 Life Outreach International and www.gatewaypeople.com

"Forgiven and Set Free" by Linda Cochrane copyright 1986, 1991, 1996 by Care Net Published by Baker Books, a division of Baker Publishing Group P.O. Box 6287 Grand Rapids, MI 49516-6287 recommended with permission by the author.

Melissa Ohden's testimony:
http://www.youtube.com/watch?v=3adLns91_SQ &feature=related

"Breaking Free: Making Liberty in Christ a Reality in Your Life" by Beth Moore copyright 1999 LifeWay Press, tenth printing November 2001 LifeWay Church Resources Customer Service 127 Ninth Avenue North, Nashville TN 37234 recommended with permission by the publisher.

CPSIA information can be obtained at www.ICGtesting.com
Printed in the USA
BVOW041202181011

273891BV00001B/4/P

9 780983 476214